DK

LANGUAGE ARTS MADE EASY

2nd Grade Workbook

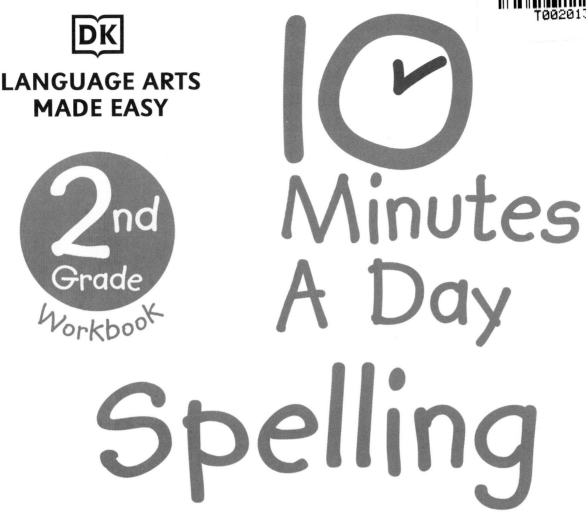

10 Minutes A Day

Spelling

Consultant Linda Ruggieri

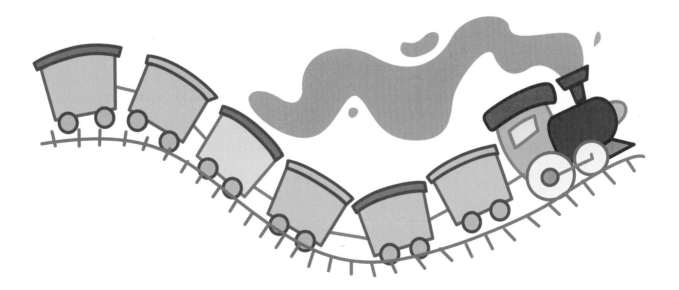

10-minute challenge

Try to complete the exercises for each topic in 10 minutes or less. Note the time it takes you in the "Time taken" column below.

Penguin Random House

DK London
Editor Elizabeth Blakemore
Senior Editor Deborah Lock
US Senior Editor Shannon Beatty
US Consultant Linda Ruggieri
Managing Editor Christine Stroyan
Managing Art Editor Anna Hall
Senior Production Editor Andy Hilliard
Senior Production Controller Jude Crozier
Jacket Design Development Manager Sophia MTT
Publisher Andrew Macintyre
Associate Publishing Director Liz Wheeler
Art Director Karen Self
Publishing Director Jonathan Metcalf

DK Delhi
Project Editor Neha Ruth Samuel
Senior Art Editor Stuti Tiwari Bhatia
Editorial Team Rohini Deb, Manjari Thakur
Art Editor Jyotsna Khosla
Managing Editors Soma B. Chowdhury, Kingshuk Ghoshal
Managing Art Editor Govind Mittal
Design Consultant Shefali Upadhyay
Senior DTP Designer Tarun Sharma
DTP Designers Sachin Gupta, Anita Yadav, Rakesh Kumar, Harish Aggarwal
Senior Jacket Designer Suhita Dharamjit
Jackets Editorial Coordinator Priyanka Sharma

This American Edition, 2020
First American Edition, 2014
Published in the United States by DK Publishing
1450 Broadway, Suite 801, New York, NY 10018

Copyright © 2014, 2020 Dorling Kindersley Limited
DK, a Division of Penguin Random House LLC
22 23 24 10 9 8 7 6 5 4 3
003–322742–May/2020

A catalog record for this book is available from the Library of Congress
ISBN 978-0-7440-3148-5

DK books are available at special discounts when purchased in bulk for sales promotions, premiums, fund-raising, or educational use. For details, contact: DK Publishing Special Markets 1450 Broadway, Suite 801, New York, NY 10018 SpecialSales@dk.com

Printed and bound in China

All images © Dorling Kindersley Limited
For further information see: www.dkimages.com

For the curious
www.dk.com

This book was made with Forest Stewardship Council™ certified paper – one small step in DK's commitment to a sustainable future. For more information go to www.dk.com/our-green-pledge

Contents

Time Taken

Time Filler:
In these boxes are some extra challenges to extend your skills. You can do them if you have some time left after finishing the questions. Or, these can be stand-alone activities that you can do in 10 minutes.

Long "a" Sound

The letter **a** is often joined with other letters to make this sound. Let's get started!

① Complete the words with one of these spelling patterns:

ay   ai   a-e

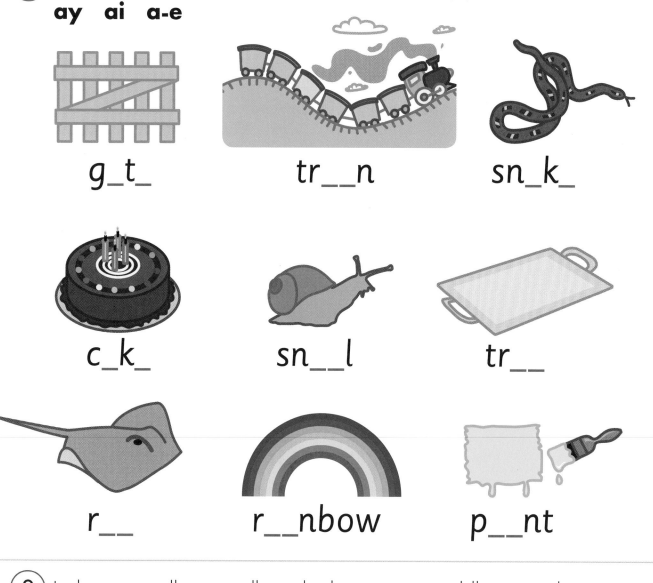

g_t_

tr__n

sn_k_

c_k_

sn__l

tr__

r__

r__nbow

p__nt

② Is the **ay** spelling usually at the beginning, middle, or end of a word?

....

Time Filler:
Can you say or write
the days of the week?
What is the date of
your birthday?

③ Circle the words with the long "a" sound.

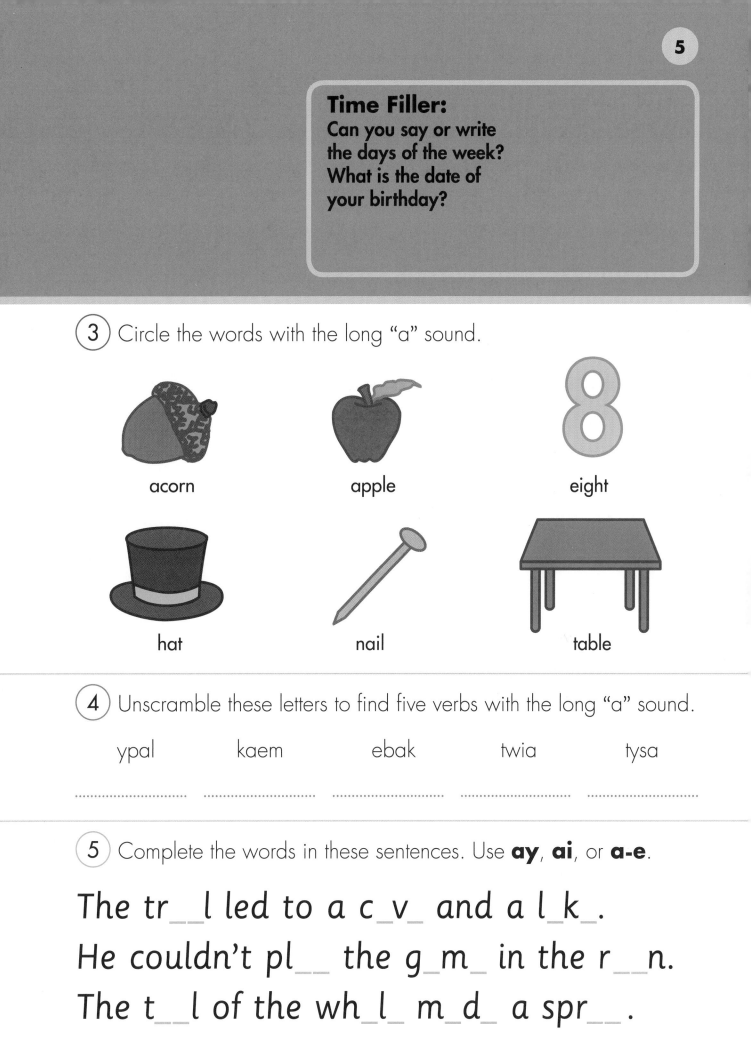

acorn

apple

eight

hat

nail

table

④ Unscramble these letters to find five verbs with the long "a" sound.

ypal   kaem   ebak   twia   tysa

....

⑤ Complete the words in these sentences. Use **ay**, **ai**, or **a-e**.

The tr__l led to a c_v_ and a l_k_.
He couldn't pl__ the g_m_ in the r__n.
The t__l of the wh_l_ m_d_ a spr__.

"ar" and "air" Sounds

The letter **a** is joined with other letters to make some other useful vowel sounds. Try them out!

(1) Complete these words with the letters **ar** to make the "ar" sound. Use the letters of the alphabet to make words that rhyme.

a b c d e f g h i j k l m n o p q r s t u v w x y z

st__ ....   c__d ....

sh__k ....   h__p ....

__t ....   f__m ....

ch__t ....   __k ....

j__ ....   y__n ....

(2) Choose a word from the box to complete each sentence.

party	artist	farmer

The .... rode on a tractor around his field.

Jake put up balloons for his ....

The .... painted a picture for the art gallery.

Time Filler:
If you find some words tricky,
you can learn some useful phrases.
To remember "pair" and "pear," learn
this sentence: you feel like you are
walking on AIR in the perfect pAIR of
shoes; a pEAr is a fruit that you EAt.

3) Say what is in each picture aloud. Each has an "air" sound.
This sound can be spelled with the letters **air**, **are**, or **ear**.
Complete these words with the correct spelling pattern.

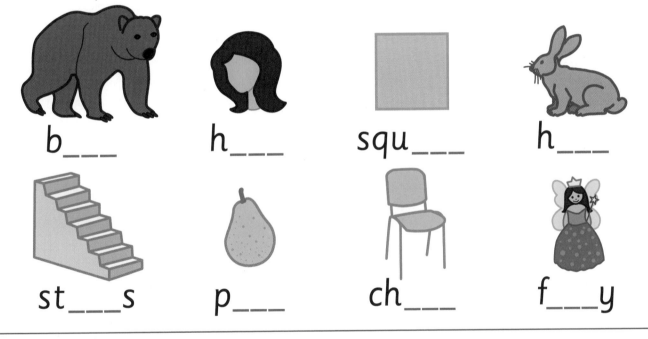

b____   h____   squ____   h____

st____s   p____   ch____   f____y

4) The spelling pattern **ere** can also make an "air" sound.
Circle the words with this sound in the passage.

"Where is the light switch?" asked Jake.

"It is over there by the door," said Jane.

5) Do you know two other words that sound like "there,"
but are spelled differently?

....

Double Letters

Consonants are sometimes doubled after a short vowel sound. Get started and double the letters.

① Complete the words by doubling the letter **b**, **d**, **f**, or **g**. Connect each word to its picture.

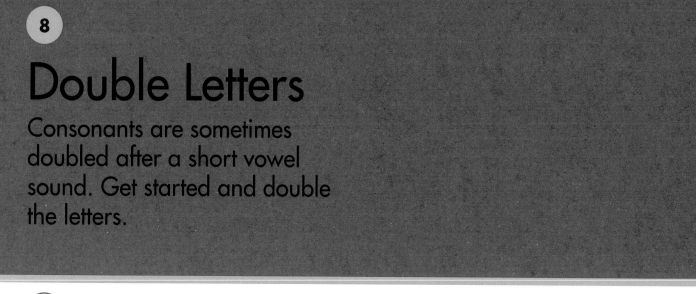

a__   ra__it   e__

da__odil   te__y   lu__age

② Complete the words by doubling the letter **l**, **m**, or **p**. Connect each word to its picture.

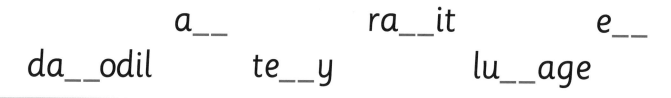

do__

be__

pu__et

ba__

fli__ers

Time Filler:
Remember the spellings of "desert" and "dessert" by learning: a deSert is full of sand with one S and a deSSert is full of Sweet Stuff.

(3) Complete the words by doubling the letter **r**, **s**, or **t**.
Connect each word to its picture.

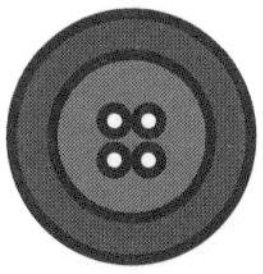

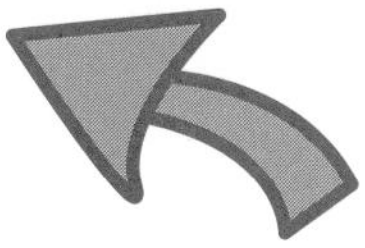

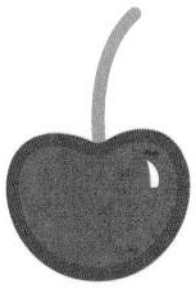

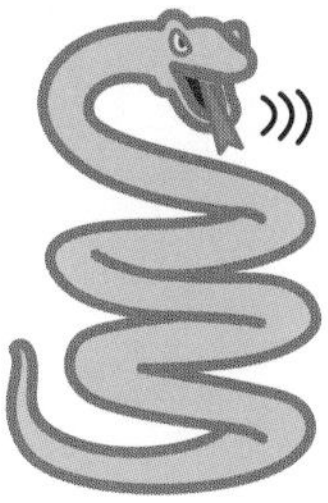

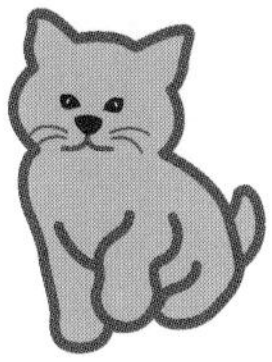

hi__

a__ow

ki__en

che__y

bu__on

(4) Complete these words with the letters **ck**.

sa__ ro__et chi__ ti__et bu__et

(5) Circle the words that **do not** follow the double-letter rule.

off bus hid wall

yes if dizzy cab

Compound Words

These words are two words
joined together without
changes to their spellings.
Can you find the two words?

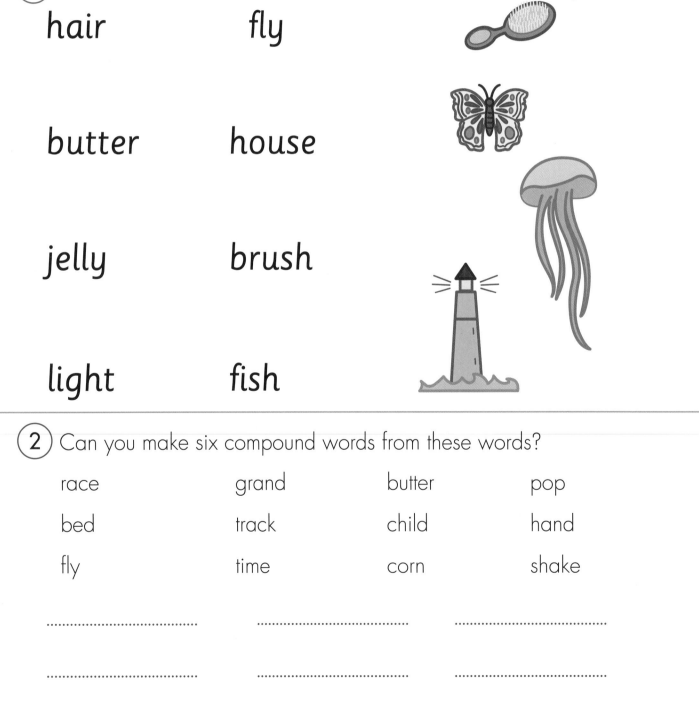

1 Connect two words to make one word. Then link each to its picture.

hair   fly

butter   house

jelly   brush

light   fish

2 Can you make six compound words from these words?

race	grand	butter	pop
bed	track	child	hand
fly	time	corn	shake

....

....

3) Make eight compound words. Use a word in the red box
and a word in the green box.

| in | out | up | down |

| doors | side | hill | stairs |

....

....

4) Split these words into two separate words. Put a line where they split.

bathroom   **firework**   **keyhole**

footprint   **pancake**

5) The word "automobile" has four syllables. How many syllables
do these words have?

skyscraper   wheelbarrow   nothing

newspaper   farmyard   tablespoon

Long "e" Sound

The most common spelling
patterns for the long "e" sound
are **ee** and **ea**. Try these pages
to see what we mean.

1 Complete these words with one of these spelling patterns:
ee   ea

f__t

__gle

s__ds

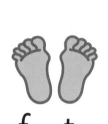

s__l

tr__

s__t

2 Complete each word with the letters **ee**. Then use
the letters of the alphabet to make words that rhyme.
a b c d e f g h i j k l m n o p q r s t u v w x y z

n__d ....

s__k ....

h__l ....

str__t ....

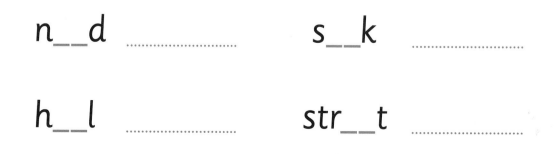

(3) Complete each word with the letters **ea**. Then use the letters of the alphabet to make words that rhyme.

a b c d e f g h i j k l m n o p q r s t u v w x y z

n__t ....

l__p ....

cr__m ....

b__st ....

(4) Say the word for each number. Circle the numbers that have an "ee" sound in the words.

3   6   9   14   18

(5) Use these words to complete the sentences.

| seasons | week | sheep | beach |

There are seven days in a ....

Tim made a sandcastle at the ....

The .... are spring, summer, fall, and winter.

The field was full of ....

"ea" or "ear" Sounds

The letter **e** is joined with other letters to make some other useful vowel sounds. Get ready, get set, go!

(1) Circle the pictures with the short "ea" sound.

eye

head

bread

feather

bird

(2) Add the letters **ea** to complete these words. Say the words aloud.

r__dy   h__vy   thr__d

w__ther   br__kfast   h__lth

(3) Complete the words with one of these spelling patterns:
eer ear

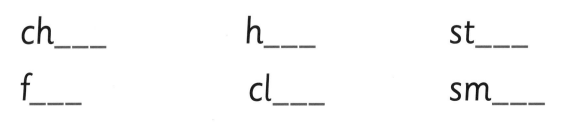

ch___   h___   st___

f___   cl___   sm___

Time Filler:
To remember the difference between "hear" and "here," learn that you hEAR with your EAR, and the position HERE is in tHERE.

4 Use the words you made in question 3 to complete the sentences.

The crowd gave a ....

Dan could .... the crowd.

The fish swam in the .... water.

The people .... the dragon.

There was a .... on the window.

5 Find these words in the word search.

peer   near   year   deadly   already   weapon

s	y	e	o	n	w	d
w	e	a	p	o	n	e
e	a	l	y	r	e	a
c	r	d	a	r	a	d
e	a	p	e	e	r	l
a	l	r	e	a	d	y

Letter Clusters

Practice blending two consonants together at the end of the word. Letters cluster together like friends.

① Add the letters **lp**, **lf**, or **lk** to complete these words.

se__   mi__   he__

su__   si__   go__

② These words end in the letters **lt** or **ld**. Link the words that rhyme.

hold   built   gold

wild

kilt   cold   felt   child

belt

mild   melt   silt

③ Choose a word from the box to complete each sentence.

colt	shelf	wolf	world

A young horse is called a ....

The book was put on the ....

The .... howled in the night.

The news was about people around the ....

(**4**) Read the words on the coins. Then sort these words
into sets by writing them on the piggy banks.

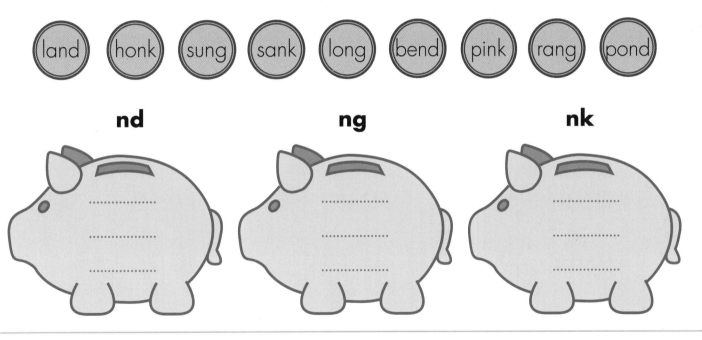

nd   **ng**   **nk**

(**5**) Change the vowel in each of these verbs to write what happened
yesterday and what will have happened by tomorrow.

Today	Yesterday (Change Vowel to **a**)	Tomorrow (Change Vowel to **u**)
sing		
ring		
sink		
drink		

Verb Endings

Add -**ed** or -**ing** to
the end of a verb to tell
when something happens.
Let's get started!

(1) Add -**ing** to each verb to tell what is happening now.

shout___   lift___   cook___

pull___   jump___   rest___

(2) Add -**ed** to each verb to tell what has happened before.

melt__   ask__   help__

land__   climb__   look__

(3) These verbs end in **e**. Drop the **e** and add -**ing** or -**ed**.

Verb	Happen**ing** Now (Add -**ing**)	Happen**ed** Before (Add -**ed**)
use		
bake		
hike		
vote		

Time Filler:
Make a list of everything you have done today. Circle the verbs. What ending have you used to write about your day?

4 When a verb has a consonant before the **y**, change **y** to **i** when adding **-ed**. Check (✔) the correct spelling.

☐ ☐
marryed or married

☐ ☐
marrying or marriing

☐ ☐
cryed or cried

☐ ☐
crying or criing

☐ ☐
enjoyed or enjoied

☐ ☐
enjoying or enjoiing

5 These verbs have a short vowel sound. Double the last consonant before adding the verb endings **-ing** or **-ed** to each word.

fit + ing = ...

spot + ed = ...

hum + ing = ...

tap + ed = ...

cut + ing = ...

rub + ed = ...

Useful Word List 1

Read each column of words. After that, cover the words up one by one and write them. Then move on to the next column.

he	....	have	....	can	....
she	....	has	....	say	....
him	....	had	....	said	....
his	....	here	....	with	....
her	....	came	....	want	....
you	....	come	....	was	....
me	....	some	....	will	....
my	....	see	....	well	....
are	....	saw	....	went	....
for	....	how	....	were	....

Time Filler:
Choose five words in this list and use each one in its own sentence. Keep coming back to these lists to check that you still know these useful words.

one	the	made
two	that	make
did	they	more
do	their	much
down	them	why
up	then	where
so	this	when
no	there	which
new	these	who
now	three	what

More Clusters

Keep an ear out for consonants
that have their own sounds,
but blend with other
consonants in words.

1) Add the letters **sp**, **sk**, or **xt** to complete these words.

ga__   ma__   ne__

de__   te__   cri__

2) These words end with the letters **nt** or **st**. Link the words that rhyme.

last   bent   nest   dent

list   fist   past

fast
west   tent   mist   best

3) Choose a word from the box to complete each sentence.

| stamp | gift | mask | beast |

Todd wore a _____ to the party.

The _____ had sharp teeth and hooked claws.

I wrapped my _____ for Dad's birthday.

A _____ goes on an envelope.

4 Read the words on the coins. Then sort these words
into sets by writing them on the piggy banks.

limp   camp   soft   wept   lift   bump   erupt   raft   kept

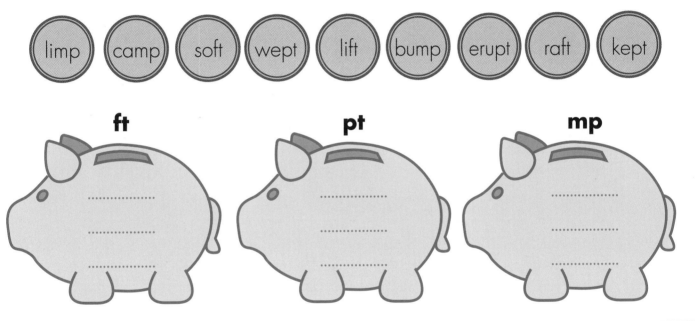

ft

pt

mp

....
....
....

....
....
....

....
....
....

5 Find these words in the word search.

grasp   jump   crept   post   wrist   stump

t	g	r	a	s	p
p	r	a	j	t	c
o	u	j	u	s	r
s	t	u	m	p	e
t	l	g	p	m	p
s	w	r	i	s	t

"er" Sound

The "er" sound has many spelling patterns, such as **er**, **ir**, and **ur**, so choose carefully.

1 Complete the words with one of these spelling patterns:

er   ir   ur

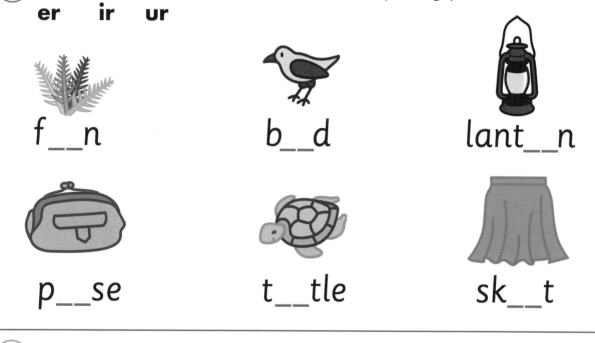

f __ __ n

b __ __ d

lant __ __ n

p __ __ se

t __ __ tle

sk __ __ t

2 Unscramble these letters to find five nouns with the "er" sound.

hrtist   ilgr   rekuty   vruce   dreh

....

3 These names of jobs end with the letters **er**. Complete the words.

teach __ __   farm __ __   danc __ __

driv __ __   build __ __   lawy __ __

Time Filler:
To remember how to spell "together,"
split it into TO GET HER and then you
will be TOGETHER. Or try splitting
it up into sound chunks: to-geth-er.
Try splitting these words up into
chunks: "wonderful" and "different."

④ Read the words. Draw a picture to show
the meaning of each word.

stir

squirt

dirty

burn

burst

shatter

⑤ Complete the words in these sentences, using **er** or **ir**.

I grew some mint in the h__b patch.

Jake took pictures with his cam__a.

The b__ds whistled and ch__ped.

Digraphs and Blends

Try out these digraphs and blends. Are you ready?
Let's do it!

1 Digraphs combine two or more letters that make one sound unlike either letter. Look at the pictures. Add the digraphs **sh** or **ch**.

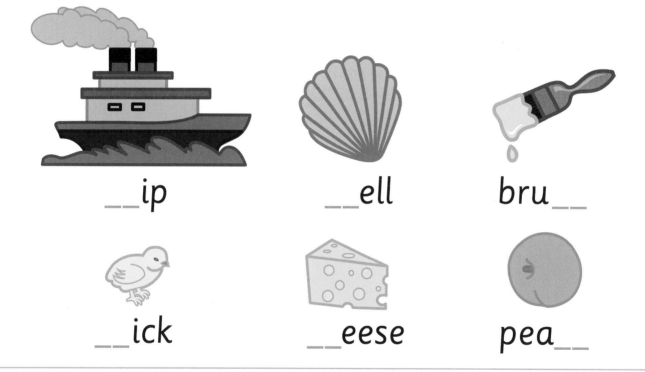

___ip   ___ell   bru___

__ick   __eese   pea__

2 Underline the "th" sound when it appears in these sentences.

The brothers were thin.

Thunder crashed around them.

Their mother and father made fresh broth.

Time Filler:
Try saying this tongue twister:
Chester chews through shoes.
Should Chester choose the
shoes he chews? Make your
own tongue twister with the
ch, **sh**, and **th** letters.

3) Blends combine two or three letters that can each be heard.
Complete these words using the blends **shr** or **thr**.

___one   ___ub   ___ob

___imp   ___oat   ___iek

4) Draw lines to link the words that rhyme.

match   lunch   fish   catch

bunch   hatch   cash   wish

dash   munch   dish

sash

5) Change the vowel sound to make a new word from each of
these words. Use **a**, **e**, **i**, **o**, or **u**.

throw   shrink   rush   bench   hutch

Compare Adjectives

Adjectives describe people, places, or things. Add -**er** or -**est** to compare them.

(1) Add -**er** to each word to compare two things.

fast__   rich__   weak__

slow__   poor__   strong__

(2) Add -**est** to each word to mean the top thing.

old___   low___   short___

young___   high___   tall___

(3) These words have a short vowel sound.
Double the last consonant before adding the endings.

Adjective	Compare Two Things (Add -**er**)	The Top Things (Add -**est**)
fit		
thin		
hot		
wet		

Time Filler:
Compare the members of your family and set some challenges. Who is the tallest, or who runs the fastest? Is there anyone smaller than you? Can you hop for longer, and who can jump the highest?

(4) These words end in **e** or **y**. Drop the **e** or change the **y** to an **i** in these words before adding -**er** or -**est**.

nice + er = ...

pretty + est = ...

wide + er = ...

large + est = ...

heavy + er = ...

tiny + est = ...

(5) Some adjectives do not follow the rules. Use these words to complete the chart.

little   better   worst   many   most   less

Adjective	Compare Two Things	The Top Things
good		best
		least
bad	worse	
	more	

Long "i" Sound

The letter **i** often joins with other letters to form the long "i" sound. But the letter **y** makes the sound, too.

① Complete these words with one of these spelling patterns:
ie   i-e

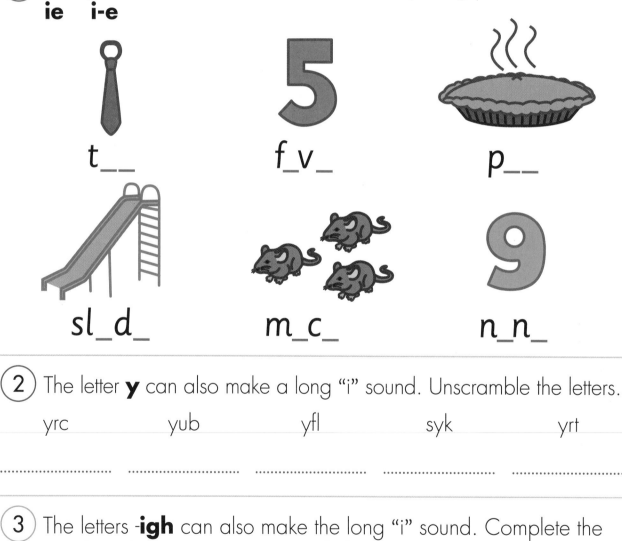

t_ _

f_v_

p_ _

sl_d_

m_c_

n_n_

② The letter **y** can also make a long "i" sound. Unscramble the letters.

yrc   yub   yfl   syk   yrt

....

③ The letters -**igh** can also make the long "i" sound. Complete the words in these sentences, using **igh**, **i-e**, **y**, or **ie**.

The br_ _ _t star sh_n_s in the n_ _ _t sk_.

The k_t_ fl_ _s h_ _ _ and d_v_s low.

Time Filler:
Write a poem about night time.
Try to use lots of words with
the long "i" sound, such as
"moonlight," "sky," and "fireflies."

④ Read the words on the bows. Then sort these words into sets
by writing them on the kites.

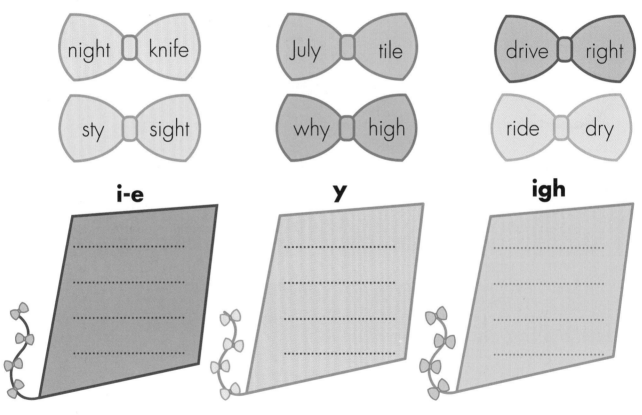

night | knife   July | tile   drive | right

sty | sight   why | high   ride | dry

i-e   **y**   **igh**

⑤ Complete these words with the long "i" sound. Then use
the letters of the alphabet to make words that rhyme.

a b c d e f g h i j k l m n o p q r s t u v w x y z

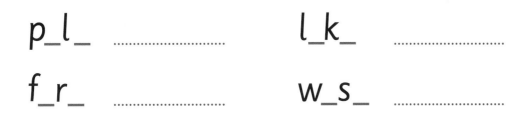

p_l_ ....   l_k_ ....

f_r_ ....   w_s_ ....

Beginning Blends

Here are some more combinations of consonants at the beginning of a word.

1 Use these beginning blends to complete the words below:

cl   pl   sl

__ock   __ant   __ide

2 In each sentence, circle the blends **bl** and **cl** at the start of words.

The black blob of ink blended on the blot.

The clock went clink, clank, clunk.

3 Unscramble these letters to find five words beginning with either **gl** or **pl**.

dgal   napl   tolp   geul   spul

....

Time Filler:
Look at the letters on car license plates. Can you think of words with those letters in them? For example, the letters PAM could make "palm" and "stamp."

④ Use these beginning blends to complete the words:

br dr fr gr pr tr

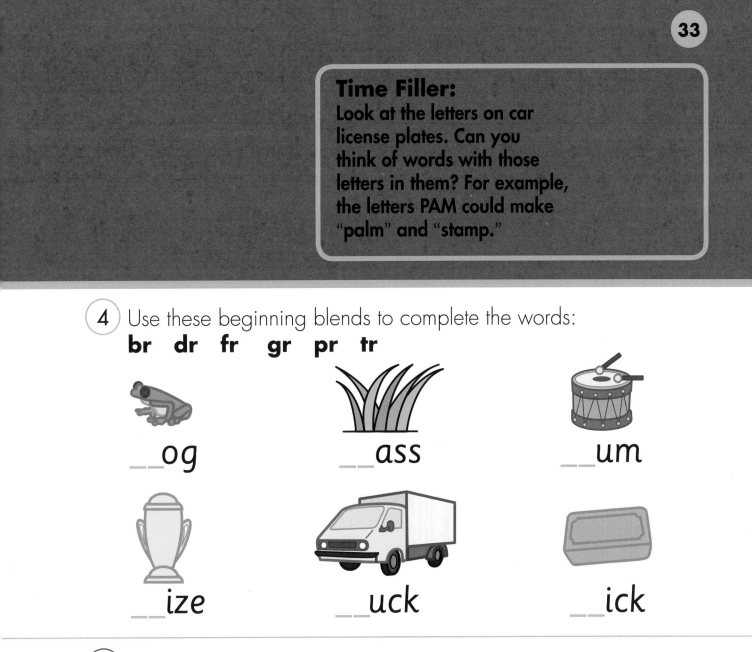

__og   __ass   __um

__ize   __uck   __ick

⑤ Read the words on the bricks. Then sort these words into sets by writing them on the walls.

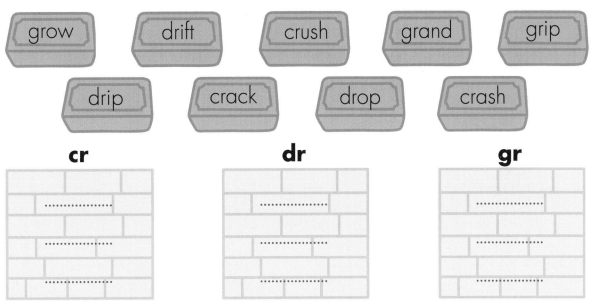

grow   drift   crush   grand   grip

drip   crack   drop   crash

cr   **dr**   **gr**

Contractions

When words combine and drop letters, an apostrophe is used to show that letters are missing. Do you think you're ready to try these?

(1) Separate each word into two words.

he's ....

you'll ....

didn't ....

I've ....

(2) Combine the two words to make one word in each case.

can not ....

you are ....

she will ....

we have ....

(3) Match each two-word form to its contraction.

could not   don't

do not   it's

I am   I'm

it is   couldn't

Time Filler:
Look through a comic book and point out the contractions. What effect do the contractions have on the way the words are spoken?

(4) For each sentence, circle the two words that can be combined. Write the contracted form of the words.

Who is coming to see the movie? ....

You are going to be late for the show. ....

What is on today? ....

We have been to the movies. ....

(5) Check (✔) the correct sentences and put an X next to any errors. Then correct the mistakes.

"Where's your book?" asked the teacher. ☐ ....

"Its at home," said Emma. ☐ ....

She'ad forgotten it. ☐ ....

"I'll bring it in tomorrow," she said. ☐ ....

Long "o" Sound

The letter **o** often joins other letters to make spelling patterns for the long "o" sound.

1. Complete these words with one of these spelling patterns:

oa   oe   o-e   ow

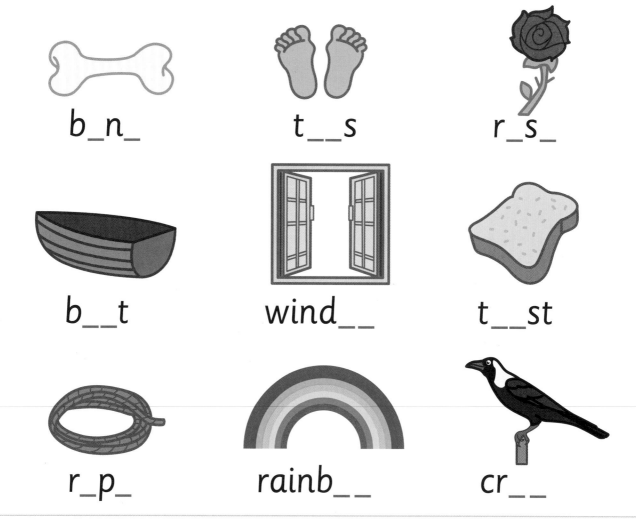

b _ n _   t _ _ s   r _ s _

b _ _ t   wind _ _   t _ _ st

r _ p _   rainb _ _   cr _ _

2. In the words above, is the **ow** spelling for the long "o" sound at the beginning, in the middle, or at the end of a word?

....

Time Filler:
A useful way to know the spelling of some tricky words is to learn a phrase that uses the letters in order. For example, for the word "ocean," remember "Only Cats' Eyes Are Narrow." Make your own phrases for words that you find tricky to spell.

③ Complete each word with the letters **oa**. Then use the letters of the alphabet to make words that rhyme with each one.

a b c d e f g h i j k l m n o p q r s t u v w x y z

s__k ....   c__ch ....

fl__t ....   c__st ....

④ Circle the words with the long "o" sound.

soap   cow   hoe   globe

⑤ Unscramble these letters to find five verbs with the long "o" sound.

keow   obwl   dola   rogw   kroca

"oy" and "ow" Sounds

Here are some more useful spelling patterns to know and use. How well will you do?

1 Circle the pictures with the "oy" and "ow" sounds.

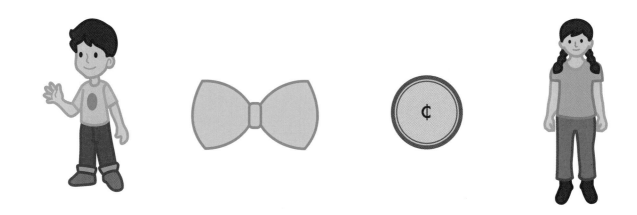

2 Add the letters **oi** to complete these words. Say the words aloud.

b__l   p__nt   n__sy

c__n   v__ce   h__st

3 Complete these words with one of these spelling patterns:
oi   oy

j__n   t__   enj__

ann__   ch__ce   r__al

Time Filler:
Go outside and make some noisy sounds: "howl," "growl," and "oink." What other noises do animals make? Keep an ear out for the vowel sounds in these words: "chirp," "screech," and "croak."

4 Complete each word with the letters **ou** or **ow**. Then use the letters of the alphabet to make words that rhyme with each one.
a b c d e f g h i j k l m n o p q r s t u v w x y z

cr _ _ n _____   all _ _ _____

m _ _ th _____   cl _ _ d _____

h _ _ l _____   h _ _ se _____

fl _ _ er _____   f _ _ nd _____

5 Use these words to complete the sentences below.

| loud | mouse | outside | crowd |

The _____ gave a cheer and waved flags.

The music was very _____ at the concert.

A _____ is a small animal.

When it started to rain _____, everyone ran inside.

Tricky Letters

Some words have consonant digraphs (**wh**), and you may not clearly hear each letter sound. Some words have consonant blends (**tw**), and you may hear each letter. Watch out as you try these.

1 Complete these words by adding the letters **wh** or **tw**.

__eel   __ig   __istle

__ins   __elve   __ale

2 Use these words to complete the sentences.

twenty	wheat	what	twisted

The strands of hemp were _____ to make a rope.

_____ color is the flag?

_____ is written with the digits 2 and 0.

The _____ was made into bread.

Time Filler:
Here is a phrase to help you remember the spelling of "rhythm": Rhythm Helps Your Two Hips Move. Make some phrases for two words on this page, using one word for each letter.

(3) The letters **qu** make the "kw" sound. Match each question to its word answer.

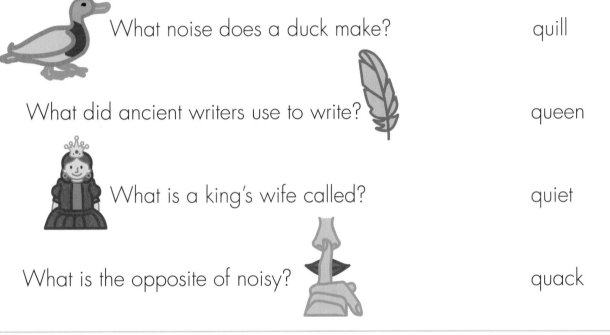

What noise does a duck make?   quill

What did ancient writers use to write?   queen

What is a king's wife called?   quiet

What is the opposite of noisy?   quack

(4) The letters **ph** make the "f" sound. Circle the letters that make the "f" sound in these words.

elephant   telephone   dolphin

(5) Which two letters make the "f" sound?   ....

Which two letters make the "kw" sound?   ....

Plurals

A plural is more than one of something. Let's change one thing to more than one.

1 If the ending of a plural sounds like "s" or "z," then add an **-s**.
If the ending has an extra syllable, then add **-es**.
Write the plural forms for these words.

cat .... box ....

rock .... glass ....

2 To make a word ending in **y** into a plural, the **y** changes to **i** when there is a consonant before the **y**. Put a check (✔) next to the correct spellings.

☐ ☐   ☐ ☐   ☐ ☐

valleys or valleies   ladys or ladies   pennys or pennies

☐ ☐   ☐ ☐   ☐ ☐

citys or cities   keys or keies   chimneys or chimneies

Can you remember the rule for when a **y** is changed to an **i**?

....

3 If a word ends in an "f" sound, change the **f** to a **v** and add **-es**.
Write the plural forms for these words.

knife .... calf ....

shelf .... leaf ....

Time Filler:
Find ten objects around your home. Use a dictionary to spell their plural forms. What spelling patterns have you used?

(4) Make the words plural by adding **-s** or **-es**. Check in a dictionary.

kangaroo .... piano ....

hero .... tomato ....

potato .... volcano ....

(5) Some words change completely from the singular to the plural form. Match each word to its correct plural.

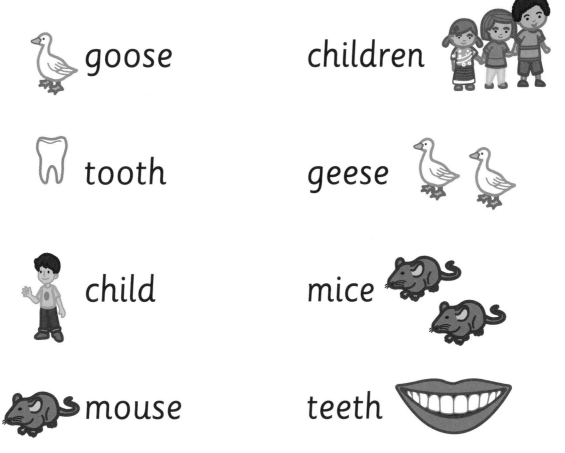

goose   children

tooth   geese

child   mice

mouse   teeth

Useful Word List 2

Read each column of words. After that, cover the words up one by one and write them. Then move on to the next column.

left	....	boy	....
right	....	girl	....
last	....	before	....
first	....	after	....
second	....	again	....
third	....	always	....
fast	....	own	....
slow	....	found	....
four	....	round	....
five	....	good	....

Time Filler:
Choose five words in this list and use each one in its own sentence. Keep coming back to these lists to check that you still know these useful words.

any	....	red	....
only	....	black	....
ask	....	blue	....
put	....	white	....
pull	....	green	....
push	....	brown	....
than	....	yellow	....
thing	....	gray	....
think	....	purple	....
thought	....	orange	....

"or" and "au" Sounds

Practice spelling words with the "or" sound, as in sh**or**t, and "au" sound, as in p**au**se. Let's go!

① Complete these words with one of these spelling patterns:

or   **oar**   **oor**   **ore**

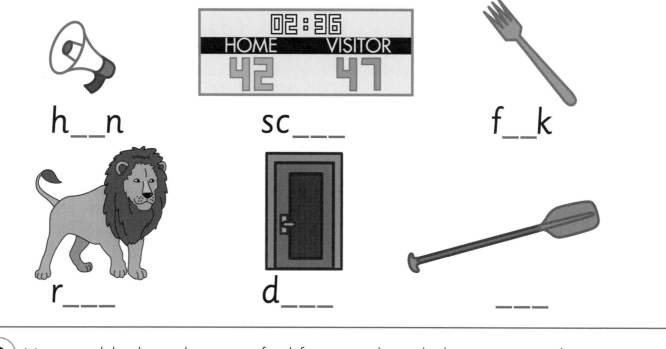

h__n

sc____

f__k

r____

d____

____

② Unscramble these letters to find five words with the "or" sound.

arro   reom   norb   trof   rlofo

....

③ Complete these words with the spelling patterns **au** or **aw**.

cl__   sh__l   __thor

p__print   str__   s__cer

Time Filler:
Here is a phrase to help you
spell "because": Big Elephants Can
Always Understand Small Elephants.
Write a sentence with "because" in it.

④ Find these words in the word search.

board   wore   crawl   sport   north   dawn

t	w	d	c	s	n
b	o	a	r	d	o
o	r	w	a	s	r
s	e	n	w	p	t
t	h	g	l	m	h
s	p	o	r	t	t

⑤ Use these words to complete the sentences below.

haunted	drawer	corners

Everybody was scared to go into the .... house.

A triangle has three ....

Liz put away her shirts in the top ....

More Beginning Blends

The letter **s** starts many consonant blends, especially at the beginning of a word.

1 Read the words on the stamps. Then sort these words into sets by writing them on the envelopes.

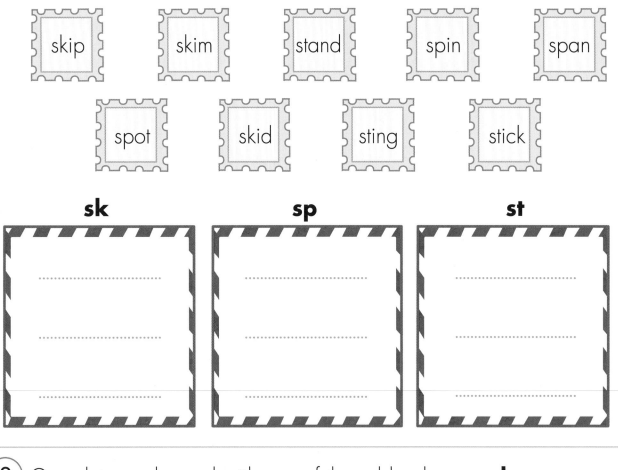

skip   skim   stand   spin   span

spot   skid   sting   stick

sk

sp

st

2 Complete each word with one of these blends: **sc   sl   sw   sm**

__an   __arf   __ing

__ell   __ift   __ile

Time Filler:
Try saying this tongue twister:
Shirley slept sweetly.
Use the words on these pages and others to make your own tongue twister with the letters **sk**, **sp**, and **st**.

(3) Circle the letter that has changed each time.

smell ~ spell ~ swell ~ swill ~ spill

snip ~ skip ~ slip ~ slim ~ skim

(4) Complete each word using the letter blends **spr**, **str**, or **scr**.
Then use the letters of the alphabet to make words that rhyme.
a b c d e f g h i j k l m n o p q r s t u v w x y z

___int .... ___ub ....

___and .... ___ong ....

(5) Match each question to its word answer.

What does an actor use?   swim

What is the noise of
a ball falling in water?   script

How does a fish move
around in water?   splash

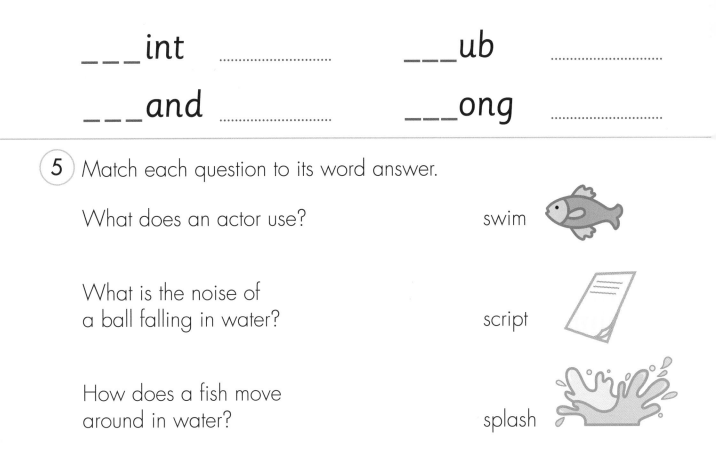

Long "oo" Sound

Listen carefully for the "oo" sound in m**oo**n, and try out the spelling patterns.

(1) Circle the words with the long "oo" sound.

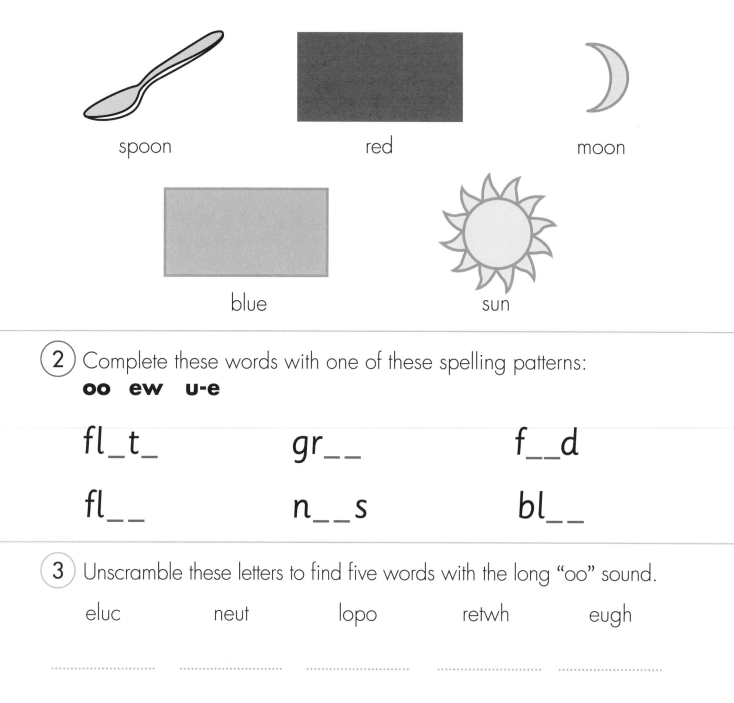

spoon

red

moon

blue

sun

(2) Complete these words with one of these spelling patterns:

oo   ew   u-e

fl_t_   gr_ _   f_ _d

fl_ _   n_ _s   bl_ _

(3) Unscramble these letters to find five words with the long "oo" sound.

eluc   neut   lopo   retwh   eugh

....

(4) Complete each word using the letter digraphs **oo** or **ue**.
Then use the letters of the alphabet to make words that rhyme.
a b c d e f g h i j k l m n o p q r s t u v w x y z

f__d .... r__t ....

gl__ .... d__ ....

s__n .... br__m ....

z__ .... h__p ....

t__l ....

(5) Choose a word from the box to complete the sentences below.

jewels	broom	true

A royal crown has many .... on it.

The statement, "The blue whale is the largest mammal," is ....

Cinderella used a .... to sweep the floor.

Short "oo" Sound

This "oo" sound is in
foot and p**u**sh. The
sound mostly comes
in the middle of a word.

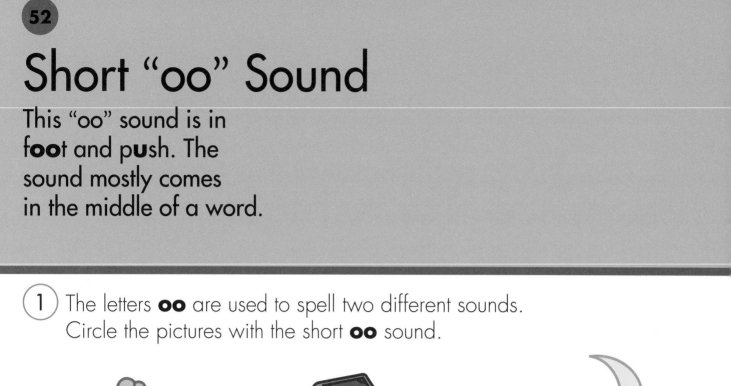

(1) The letters **oo** are used to spell two different sounds.
Circle the pictures with the short **oo** sound.

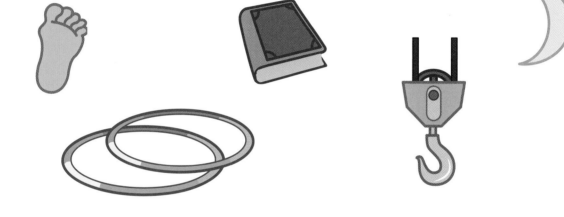

(2) Complete these words with the **oo** spelling.

l__k   st__d   w__d

br__k   t__k   w__l

(3) The "oo" sound in g**oo**d and w**oo**d is also heard in words
with the vowels **ou**. Write a sentence for each word below.

could   ....

should   ....

would   ....

Time Filler:
Write the months of the year in order, and then sort them alphabetically.

(4) Find these words in the word search.

shook   hood   good   cook   soot

brook   foot   wood   crook   book

s	g	c	a	z	i	e
h	o	o	d	f	c	y
o	o	o	u	o	r	p
o	d	k	w	o	o	d
k	s	o	o	t	o	q
j	b	r	o	o	k	a
b	o	o	k	w	e	m

(5) Use the letter **u** to make the short "oo" sound in each word.

p_ll   p_sh   s_gar

b_sh   f_ll   b_ll

Silent Letters

In some words, certain letters are
used but not sounded out and have
no effect on the rest of the word.
Can you find them?

(1) Match each picture to the letters its word begins with.

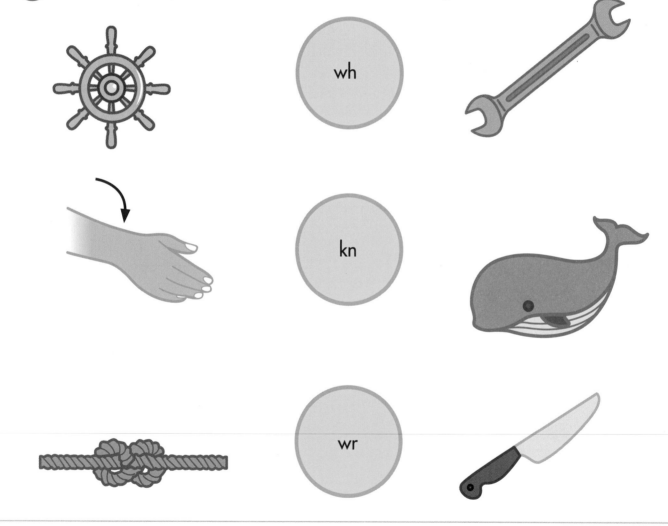

wh

kn

wr

(2) Underline the letters that are silent in these words.

knit   wrist   guard   sign

write   gnash   knee   knife

Time Filler:
Here is a phrase to help you spell "Wednesday": WE Do Not Eat Soup on WEDNESdays. How many words, with two or more letters, can you make with the letters in Wednesday?

(3) Use the letter combinations **mn** or **mb** to complete these words.

hy__   cli__   la__

colu__   thu__   sole__

(4) Use these words to complete the sentences.

| wrong | guests | kneels | crumbs |

The priest .... to pray.

Jen gave the .... from the bread to the birds.

The math sum was .... and marked with an X.

The hotel had room for 50 ....

(5) Underline the silent letters in these words.

wriggle   wreath   knock

whistle   guitar   island

Prefixes and Suffixes

A prefix is a part of a word added to its beginning and a suffix, to its end. They change the word's meaning.

1 Add the prefix **un-** to the beginning of each of these words.

__happy   __do   __load

__fair   __lock   __wrap

What do you think the prefix **un-** means? ....

2 Add the suffix **-less** to the ends of these words.

hope____   rest____   end____

tire____   speech____   age____

What do you think the suffix **-less** means? ....

3 Complete these words.

enjoy + ment = ...   sad + ness = ...

punish + ment = ...   fit + ness = ...

agree + ment = ...   dark + ness = ...

pay + ment = ...   ill + ness = ...

Time Filler:
Use a dictionary to find the meanings of five words on these pages. How has the prefix or suffix changed each word's meaning?

④ Add the suffix **-ful** to the ends of these words.

use___   cheer___   pain___

wonder___   care___   mind___

What do you think the suffix **-ful** means? ....

⑤ Combine a word from the red box with a word part from the green box to make 10 new words.

| joy | play | glad | open | help | power | cover |

| un- | -less | -ful | -ness |

Count the syllables for each of your new words.

.... ☐   .... ☐

.... ☐   .... ☐

.... ☐   .... ☐

.... ☐   .... ☐

.... ☐   .... ☐

The Letter y

Watch out for the
letter **y** because it makes
different letter sounds.
Have a try!

① The letter **y** makes a long "e" sound at the end of a word.
Add a **y** to complete these words.

bab_   famil_   hone_

② The letter **y** makes a long "i" sound when there are no other
vowels in the word. Rearrange these letters to write words.

kys   yhw   rcy   ylf   ryf

....

③ Check (✔) in the correct box to show what sound the **y** makes.

Word	Long "e" Sound	Long "i" Sound
body		
type		
empty		
shy		

Time Filler:
Read a few books and look out for the words ending in **y**. What sound does the letter **y** make? Keep a spelling diary and write the words into this.

4) The letter **y** can also make a long "a" sound and a short "i" sound. Find these words in the word search.

they   prey   cylinder   pyramid   syrup   crystal   myth   gym

s	p	h	t	g	y	m	c
c	y	l	i	n	d	e	r
p	r	e	y	u	t	s	y
d	a	y	m	a	h	p	s
l	m	s	y	r	u	p	t
y	i	p	t	h	e	y	a
c	d	l	h	t	y	g	l

5) For plurals, if the **y** follows a consonant, then change the **y** to an **i**, and add **-es**. Check (✔) the correct plural.

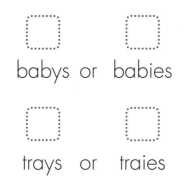

babys or babies

trays or traies

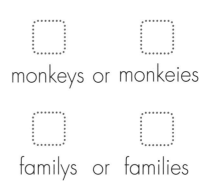

monkeys or monkeies

familys or families

"j" and "l" Sounds

Some consonant sounds have more than one spelling pattern.

(1) The letter **j** is never used at the end of a word. Instead, the "j" sound is spelled with -**dge** after the short vowel sounds and -**ge** after all other sounds. Complete these words using the spelling patterns **dge** or **ge**.

ca__   bri____   he____

(2) Complete these words with **dge** or **ge**.
Then use the words to fill in the sentences.

hu__   char__   le___   fu___   villa__

The bird sat on the window_____.

The cell phone was on _____.

The baker made a _____ birthday cake flavored with _____.

Everyone in the _____ was excited about the mayor's visit.

(3) Often when the "j" sound comes before **e**, **i**, or **y**,
the letter **g** is used. Complete these words using **j** or **g**.

_em   _uice   _iraffe   _elly

(4) The "l" sound at the end of a word has either an **-le** or **-el** spelling.
Check (✔) the words that have been spelled correctly.

☐ single   ☐ jungel   ☐ parcel   ☐ simpel

☐ towle   ☐ label   ☐ kennel   ☐ candle

(5) Complete these words with **-al** or **-il**.

penc__   sand__   utens__

anim__   foss__   pet__

Homophones and Homographs

Make sure you pay attention because some words can be very similar.

1 Homophones are words that sound the same but are spelled differently. Link the homophones.

won   see   I   write   real   hear

right   here   sea   one   eye   reel

2 Complete the sentences using these words.

to	too	two	there	their	they're

A letter was sent .... the man.

.... were .... trees in the garden.

The children read .... books.

The teacher read her book, ...

.... reading about monkeys.

3 Draw two pictures for each word.

bat

glasses

ring

Time Filler:
Design your own homophone poster with drawings for these words: "meat" and "meet," "one" and "won," and "blue" and "blew."

4 Two words that are spelled the same but have different meanings are called homographs. Look at the words in the box. Write them under the pictures.

| bark | bowl | match | sink |

....

....

5 Read the words in the box. Think of the homophone for each word, and write it under each picture.

| blew | hair | night | which |

....

Useful Word List 3

Read each column of words. After that, cover the words up one by one and write them. Then move on to the next column.

could	....	Monday	....
should	....	Tuesday	....
would	....	Wednesday	....
very	....	Thursday	....
every	....	Friday	....
other	....	Saturday	....
another	....	Sunday	....
because	....	today	....
open	....	tomorrow	....
close	....	yesterday	....

Time Filler:
Choose five words in this list and use each one in its own sentence. Keep coming back to these lists to check that you still know these useful words.

January	November
February	December
March	month
April	year
May	school
June	rain
July	cloud
August	snow
September	wind
October	weather

Answers:

4–5 Long "a" Sound
6–7 "ar" and "air" Sounds

4

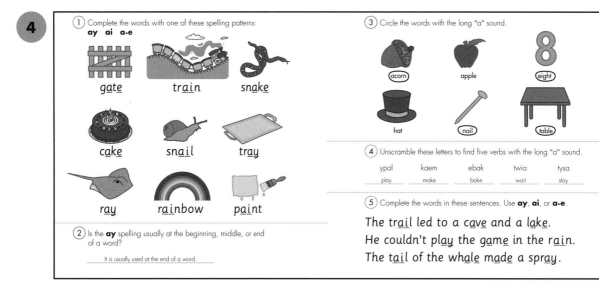

① Complete the words with one of these spelling patterns:
ay ai a-e

gate   train   snake

cake   snail   tray

ray   rainbow   paint

② Is the **ay** spelling usually at the beginning, middle, or end of a word?

It is usually used at the end of a word.

5

③ Circle the words with the long "a" sound.

(acorn)   apple   (eight)

hat   (nail)   (table)

④ Unscramble these letters to find five verbs with the long "a" sound.

ypal   kaem   ebak   twia   tysa
play   make   bake   wait   stay

⑤ Complete the words in these sentences. Use **ay**, **ai**, or **a-e**.

The trail led to a cave and a lake.
He couldn't play the game in the rain.
The tail of the whale made a spray.

By this stage children will be able to distinguish between hearing long and short vowel sounds and be aware that the long vowel sounds are represented by more than one spelling pattern.

These pages reinforce three of the most frequently used spelling patterns representing the long "a" sound, including the vowel + final -**e**.

6

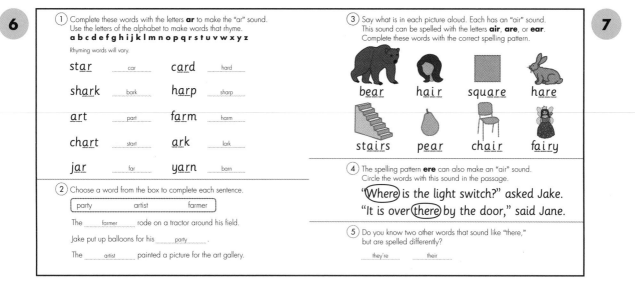

① Complete these words with the letters **ar** to make the "ar" sound. Use the letters of the alphabet to make words that rhyme.
a b c d e f g h i j k l m n o p q r s t u v w x y z

Rhyming words will vary.

star   car   card   hard

shark   bark   harp   sharp

art   part   farm   harm

chart   start   ark   lark

jar   far   yarn   barn

② Choose a word from the box to complete each sentence.

| party | artist | farmer |

The ____farmer____ rode on a tractor around his field.

Jake put up balloons for his ____party____.

The ____artist____ painted a picture for the art gallery.

7

③ Say what is in each picture aloud. Each has an "air" sound. This sound can be spelled with the letters **air**, **are**, or **ear**. Complete these words with the correct spelling pattern.

bear   hair   square   hare

stairs   pear   chair   fairy

④ The spelling pattern **ere** can also make an "air" sound. Circle the words with this sound in the passage.

"(Where) is the light switch?" asked Jake.
"It is over (there) by the door," said Jane.

⑤ Do you know two other words that sound like "there," but are spelled differently?

they're   their

Children should know that in the majority of words every syllable must have a vowel sound. However, they will be beginning to recognize the use of other common vowel sounds, such as "ar" and "air." Just

as for other vowel sounds, there are often more than one spelling pattern and these are practiced on these green pages.

Answers:

8–9 Double Letters
10–11 Compound Words

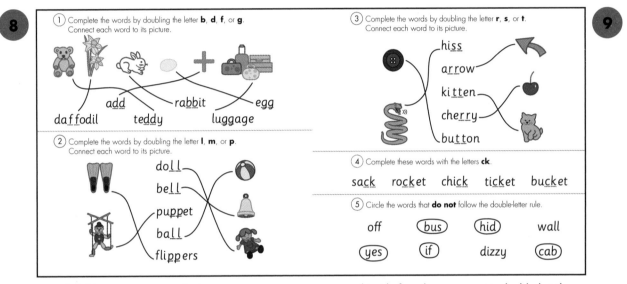

Extend children's awareness of when some consonants are doubled by asking them to say the words and listen out for the vowel sound. They will notice that there is a short "a," "e," "i," "o," or "u" sound just before the consonant is doubled. When reading, encourage children to look out for words with doubled letters. They will notice that the letters **f**, **l**, **s**, and **z** are doubled at the end of words.

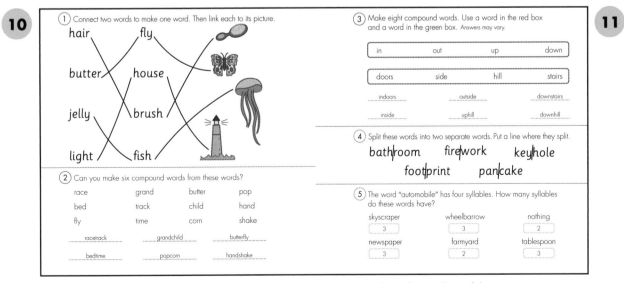

Children often enjoy joining complete words together to make compound words or finding where the two words split. A useful spelling tip is to break long words down into syllables and then work out the spelling of these more manageable chunks of letters. Can your child think of other compound words they are familiar with?

68

Answers:

12-13 Long "e" Sound
14-15 "ea" or "ear" Sounds

12

1 Complete these words with one of these spelling patterns:
ee ea

f<u>ee</u>t   <u>ea</u>gle   s<u>ee</u>ds

s<u>ea</u>l   tr<u>ee</u>   s<u>ea</u>t

2 Complete each word with the letters **ee**. Then use the letters of the alphabet to make words that rhyme.
a b c d e f g h i j k l m n o p q r s t u v w x y z
Rhyming words will vary.

n<u>ee</u>d   seed   s<u>ee</u>k   creek

h<u>ee</u>l   reel   str<u>ee</u>t   beat

3 Complete each word with the letters **ea**. Then use the letters of the alphabet to make words that rhyme.
a b c d e f g h i j k l m n o p q r s t u v w x y z
Rhyming words will vary.

n<u>ea</u>t   feet   l<u>ea</u>p   keep

cr<u>ea</u>m   steam   b<u>ea</u>st   feast

4 Say the word for each number. Circle the numbers that have an "ee" sound in the words.

(3)   6   9   (14)   (18)

5 Use these words to complete the sentences.

| seasons | week | sheep | beach |

There are seven days in a ___week___.

Tim made a sandcastle at the ___beach___.

The ___seasons___ are spring, summer, fall, and winter.

The field was full of ___sheep___.

13

These orange pages indicate practice with the various spelling patterns that make a specific long vowel sound. Help children by explaining that words that sound the same can be spelled differently and have different meanings, such as "been" and "bin." For the Time Filler, children's poems do not need to rhyme, but they may find that they use plenty of words that do.

14

1 Circle the pictures with the short "ea" sound.

eye   head   bread   feather   bird

2 Add the letters **ea** to complete these words. Say the words aloud.

r<u>ea</u>dy   h<u>ea</u>vy   thr<u>ea</u>d
w<u>ea</u>ther   br<u>ea</u>kfast   h<u>ea</u>lth

3 Complete the words with one of these spelling patterns:
eer ear

ch<u>eer</u>   h<u>ear</u>   st<u>eer</u>
f<u>ear</u>   cl<u>ear</u>   sm<u>ear</u>

4 Use the words you made in question 3 to complete the sentences.

The crowd gave a ___cheer___.
Dan could ___hear___ the crowd.
The fish swam in the ___clear___ water.
The people ___fear___ the dragon.
There was a ___smear___ on the window.

5 Find these words in the word search.

peer   near   year   deadly   already   weapon

s	y	e	o	n	w	d
w	e	a	p	o	n	e
e	a	l	y	r	e	a
c	r	d	a	r	a	d
e	a	p	e	e	r	l
a	l	r	e	a	d	y

15

If children are finding it tricky to decide which pattern to use, encourage them to write down the options and identify visually the correct spelling or use a dictionary to check. Some children will particularly rely on their visual memory of the shape of a word and the pattern of its letters to help them remember how to spell it.

Answers:

16–17 Letter Clusters
18–19 Verb Endings

 16

① Add the letters **lp**, **lf**, or **lk** to complete these words.

se<u>lf</u>   mi<u>lk</u>   he<u>lp</u>

su<u>lk</u>   si<u>lk</u>   go<u>lf</u>

② These words end in the letters **lt** or **ld**. Link the words that rhyme.

hold   wild   built   gold
kilt   cold   felt   child
belt   mild   melt   silt

③ Choose a word from the box to complete each sentence.

| colt | shelf | wolf | world |

A young horse is called a ___colt___ .

The book was put on the ___shelf___ .

The ___wolf___ howled in the night.

The news was about people around the ___world___ .

17

④ Read the words on the coins. Then sort these words into sets by writing them on the piggy banks.

land honk sung sank long bend pink rang pond

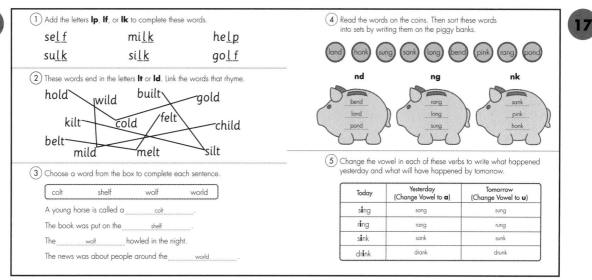

nd
bend
land
pond

ng
rang
long
sung

nk
sank
pink
honk

⑤ Change the vowel in each of these verbs to write what happened yesterday and what will have happened by tomorrow.

Today	Yesterday (Change Vowel to **a**)	Tomorrow (Change Vowel to **u**)
sing	sang	sung
ring	rang	rung
sink	sank	sunk
drink	drank	drunk

The red pages provide many examples to practice how consonants blend together in words. Encourage children to think of others words with the blends with the letter **l** in them. Also point out

to children that sometimes consonants join together to make one sound, such as "ng." Being familiar with alphabetical order will help with using the dictionary, indexes, and glossaries.

18

① Add **-ing** to each verb to tell what is happening now.

shout<u>ing</u>   lift<u>ing</u>   cook<u>ing</u>

pull<u>ing</u>   jump<u>ing</u>   rest<u>ing</u>

② Add **-ed** to each verb to tell what has happened before.

melt<u>ed</u>   ask<u>ed</u>   help<u>ed</u>

land<u>ed</u>   climb<u>ed</u>   look<u>ed</u>

③ These verbs end in **e**. Drop the **e** and add **-ing** or **-ed**.

Verb	Happen**ing** Now (Add **-ing**)	Happen**ed** Before (Add **-ed**)
use	using	used
bake	baking	baked
hike	hiking	hiked
vote	voting	voted

19

④ When a verb has a consonant before the **y**, change **y** to **i** when adding **-ed**. Check (✔) the correct spelling.

☐ marryed or ✔ married   ✔ marrying or ☐ marriing

☐ cryed or ✔ cried   ✔ crying or ☐ criing

✔ enjoyed or ☐ enjoied   ✔ enjoying or ☐ enjoiing

⑤ These verbs have a short vowel sound. Double the last consonant before adding the verb endings **-ing** or **-ed** to each word.

fit + ing = ___fitting___   spot + ed = ___spotted___

hum + ing = ___humming___   tap + ed = ___tapped___

cut + ing = ___cutting___   rub + ed = ___rubbed___

Make sure your child understands that a verb is an action word. A sentence is made complete by having a verb. The verb ending **-ing** always adds an extra syllable to a word and **-ed** sometimes does. The past tense of some verbs may sound as

if it ends in "id," "d," or "t" but all these sounds are spelled **ed**. These pages provide practice on applying spelling rules when these endings are added to words.

Answers:

22–23 More Clusters

24–25 "er" Sound

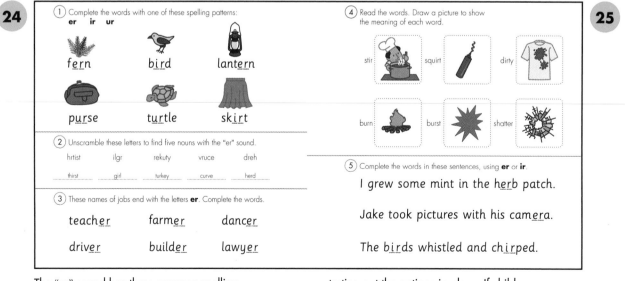

22

① Add the letters **sp**, **sk**, or **xt** to complete these words.

ga<u>sp</u>   ma<u>sk</u>   ne<u>xt</u>

de<u>sk</u>   te<u>xt</u>   cri<u>sp</u>

② These words end with the letters **nt** or **st**. Link the words that rhyme.

last   bent   nest   dent
list   fist   past
west   fast   tent   mist   best

③ Choose a word from the box to complete each sentence.

stamp	gift	mask	beast

Todd wore a ___mask___ to the party.

The ___beast___ had sharp teeth and hooked claws.

I wrapped my ___gift___ for Dad's birthday.

A ___stamp___ goes on an envelope.

23

④ Read the words on the coins. Then sort these words into sets by writing them on the piggy banks.

limp camp soft wept lift bump erupt raft kept

ft
soft
lift
raft

pt
kept
wept
erupt

mp
bump
camp
limp

⑤ Find these words in the word search.

grasp   jump   crept   post   wrist   stump

t	g	r	a	s	p
p	r	a	j	t	c
o	u	j	u	s	r
s	t	u	m	p	e
t	l	g	p	m	p
s	w	r	i	s	t

These pages practice further consonant combinations at the ends of words. There are a variety of activities for the knowledge to be reinforced in different ways: selecting the correct letters to complete the words, listening for words that rhyme, using the words in the context of a sentence, and looking closely for the letters in a word search.

24

① Complete the words with one of these spelling patterns:
er   ir   ur

f<u>er</u>n   b<u>ir</u>d   lant<u>er</u>n

p<u>ur</u>se   t<u>ur</u>tle   sk<u>ir</u>t

② Unscramble these letters to find five nouns with the "er" sound.

hrtist   ilgr   rekuty   vruce   dreh
thirst   girl   turkey   curve   herd

③ These names of jobs end with the letters **er**. Complete the words.

teach<u>er</u>   farm<u>er</u>   danc<u>er</u>

driv<u>er</u>   build<u>er</u>   lawy<u>er</u>

25

④ Read the words. Draw a picture to show the meaning of each word.

stir   squirt   dirty

burn   burst   shatter

⑤ Complete the words in these sentences, using **er** or **ir**.

I grew some mint in the h<u>er</u>b patch.

Jake took pictures with his cam<u>er</u>a.

The b<u>ir</u>ds whistled and ch<u>ir</u>ped.

The "er" sound has three common spelling patterns, and children will need to choose the right combination. They will either use their previous knowledge of seeing the word or by testing out the options in place. If children are struggling to unscramble the words, encourage them to find the spelling pattern and then see what letters are left to put around it.

Answers:

26–27 Digraphs and Blends
28–29 Compare Adjectives

26

① Digraphs combine two or more letters that make one sound unlike either letter. Look at the pictures. Add the digraphs **sh** or **ch**.

ship   shell   bru**sh**

chick   cheese   pea**ch**

② Underline the "th" sound when it appears in these sentences.

<u>Th</u>e bro<u>th</u>ers were <u>th</u>in.

<u>Th</u>under crashed around <u>th</u>em.

<u>Th</u>eir mo<u>th</u>er and fa<u>th</u>er made fresh bro<u>th</u>.

27

③ Blends combine two or three letters that can each be heard. Complete these words using the blends **shr** or **thr**.

<u>thr</u>one   <u>shr</u>ub   <u>thr</u>ob

<u>shr</u>imp   <u>thr</u>oat   <u>shr</u>iek

④ Draw lines to link the words that rhyme.

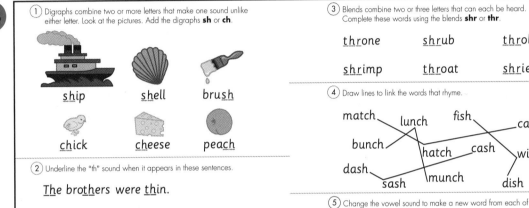

match   lunch   fish   catch
bunch   hatch   cash   wish
dash   sash   munch   dish

⑤ Change the vowel sound to make a new word from each of these words. Use **a**, **e**, **i**, **o**, or **u**. Answers may vary.

throw	shrink	rush	bench	hutch
threw	shrank	rash	bunch	hatch

The letter combinations on these pages make digraphs and blends. Tongue twisters are a fun way of becoming familiar with saying the sounds at the beginning and ends of words.

Extend the Time Filler further by asking children to identify the words that rhyme and to note how they are spelled using different letter combinations.

28

① Add **-er** to each word to compare two things.

fast**er**   rich**er**   weak**er**

slow**er**   poor**er**   strong**er**

② Add **-est** to each word to mean the top thing.

old**est**   low**est**   short**est**

young**est**   high**est**   tall**est**

③ These words have a short vowel sound. Double the last consonant before adding the endings.

Adjective	Compare Two Things (Add -er)	The Top Things (Add -est)
fit	fitter	fittest
thin	thinner	thinnest
hot	hotter	hottest
wet	wetter	wettest

29

④ These words end in **e** or **y**. Drop the **e** or change the **y** to an **i** in these words before adding **-er** or **-est**.

nice + er = nicer   pretty + est = prettiest

wide + er = wider   large + est = largest

heavy + er = heavier   tiny + est = tiniest

⑤ Some adjectives do not follow the rules. Use these words to complete the chart.

little	better	worst	many	most	less

Adjective	Compare Two Things	The Top Things
good	better	best
little	less	least
bad	worse	worst
many	more	most

Check that children know that an adjective is a word that describes a person, place, or thing. Like for adding verb endings (see page 18), there are additional rules to know when adding these adjective endings to words with a short vowel sound or end in **e** or **y**. Children need to be aware of the words that do not follow the rules. Support children by suggesting sentences that these words are used in.

Answers:

30–31 Long "i" Sound

32–33 Beginning Blends

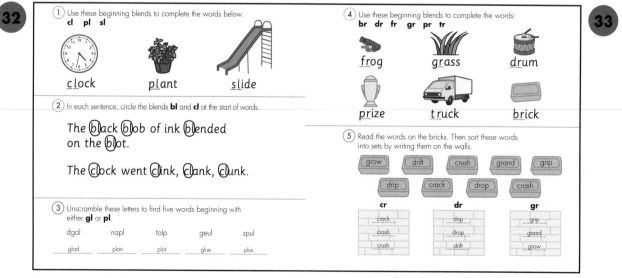

30

① Complete these words with one of these spelling patterns:
ie   i-e

t**ie**   f**i**v**e**   p**ie**

sl**i**de   m**i**ce   n**i**ne

② The letter **y** can also make a long "i" sound. Unscramble the letters.

yrc   yub   yfl   syk   yrt

cry   buy   fly   sky   try

③ The letters **-igh** can also make the long "i" sound. Complete the words in these sentences, using **igh**, **i-e**, **y**, or **ie**.

The br**igh**t star sh**i**nes in the n**igh**t sky.

The k**i**te fl**ie**s h**igh** and d**i**ves low.

31

④ Read the words on the bows. Then sort these words into sets by writing them on the kites.

night | knife   July | tile   drive | right
sty | sight   why | high   ride | dry

i-e
tile
ride
knife
drive

y
sty
July
why
dry

igh
right
sight
night
high

⑤ Complete these words with the long "i" sound. Then use the letters of the alphabet to make words that rhyme.
a b c d e f g h i j k l m n o p q r s t u v w x y z
Rhyming words will vary.

p**i**le   file   l**i**ke   strike

f**i**re   tire   w**i**se   rise

The long "i" sound has four common spelling patterns: **ie**, **i** + final **e**, **igh**, and the letter **y**. Answers will vary for the rhymes children will suggest for question 5. The answers do not need to use the same spelling pattern, for example "pies" as a rhyme for "wise." The first step to writing the poem is to compile a list of words to use. Encourage your child to read it aloud when completed.

32

① Use these beginning blends to complete the words below:
cl   pl   sl

clock   **pl**ant   **sl**ide

② In each sentence, circle the blends **bl** and **cl** at the start of words.

The (bl)ack (bl)ob of ink (bl)ended on the (bl)ot.

The (cl)ock went (cl)ink, (cl)ank, (cl)unk.

③ Unscramble these letters to find five words beginning with either **gl** or **pl**.

dgal   napl   tolp   geul   spul

glad   plan   plot   glue   plus

33

④ Use these beginning blends to complete the words:
br   dr   fr   gr   pr   tr

frog   **gr**ass   **dr**um

prize   **tr**uck   **br**ick

⑤ Read the words on the bricks. Then sort these words into sets by writing them on the walls.

grow   drift   crush   grand   grip
drip   crack   drop   crash

cr
crack
crash
crush

dr
drip
drop
drift

gr
grip
grand
grow

These activities look at consonants that combine with **l** and **r** at the beginning of words. Encourage children to read aloud the sentences in question 2 or repeat them after you. The Time Filler suggests a fun game that can be played out and about. When your child is more confident this game can be developed by the letters having to be used in the same order as well.

Answers:

34–35 Contractions
36–37 Long "o" Sound

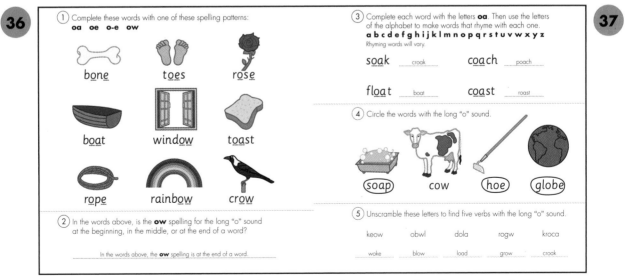

34

1 Separate each word into two words.

he's	he is
you'll	you will
didn't	did not
I've	I have

2 Combine the two words to make one word in each case.

can not	can't
you are	you're
she will	she'll
we have	we've

3 Match each two-word form to its contraction.

could not — couldn't
do not — don't
I am — I'm
it is — it's

35

4 For each sentence, circle the two words that can be combined. Write the contracted form of the words.

(Who is) coming to see the movie? — Who's

(You are) going to be late for the show. — You're

(What is) on today? — What's

(We have) been to the movies. — We've

5 Check (✔) the correct sentences and put an X next to any errors. Then correct the mistakes.

"Where's your book?" asked the teacher. ✔

"Its at home," said Emma. X — It's

She'ad forgotten it. X — She'd

"I'll bring it in tomorrow," she said. ✔

Through reading, speaking, and listening, children will become aware that sometimes two words are joined together and shortened with letters left out. These are known as contractions and an apostrophe is used to indicate where the letter or letters have been taken out. This often happens with words next to pronouns, such as "I," "we," and "you."

36

1 Complete these words with one of these spelling patterns:
oa   oe   o-e   ow

bone   toes   rose

boat   window   toast

rope   rainbow   crow

2 In the words above, is the **ow** spelling for the long "o" sound at the beginning, in the middle, or at the end of a word?

In the words above, the **ow** spelling is at the end of a word.

37

3 Complete each word with the letters **oa**. Then use the letters of the alphabet to make words that rhyme with each one.
a b c d e f g h i j k l m n o p q r s t u v w x y z
Rhyming words will vary.

soak — croak   coach — poach

float — boat   coast — roast

4 Circle the words with the long "o" sound.

(soap)   cow   (hoe)   (globe)

5 Unscramble these letters to find five verbs with the long "o" sound.

keow	obwl	dola	rogw	kroca
woke	blow	load	grow	croak

There are four common spelling patterns for the long "o" sound for children to recognize and use. As spelling is tricky, splitting words into sound chunks or learning a phrase or rhyme using the letters in the word is a helpful prompt to remember.

There are a number of examples in the Time Fillers throughout this book, but you should also encourage your child to think of their own mnemonics for words they find tricky to spell.

Answers:

38–39 "oy" and "ow" Sounds
40–41 Tricky Letters

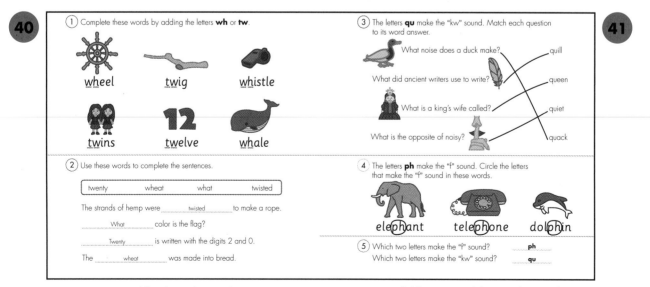

38

1. Circle the pictures with the "oy" and "ow" sounds.

2. Add the letters **oi** to complete these words. Say the words aloud.

b<u>oi</u>l   p<u>oi</u>nt   n<u>oi</u>sy

c<u>oi</u>n   v<u>oi</u>ce   h<u>oi</u>st

3. Complete these words with one of these spelling patterns:
oi   oy

j<u>oi</u>n   t<u>oy</u>   enj<u>oy</u>

ann<u>oy</u>   ch<u>oi</u>ce   r<u>oy</u>al

39

4. Complete each word with the letters **ou** or **ow**. Then use the letters of the alphabet to make words that rhyme with each one.
a b c d e f g h i j k l m n o p q r s t u v w x y z
Rhyming words will vary.

cr<u>ow</u>n ......gown......   all<u>ow</u> ......now......

m<u>ou</u>th ......south......   cl<u>ou</u>d ......loud......

h<u>ow</u>l ......owl......   h<u>ou</u>se ......mouse......

fl<u>ow</u>er ......tower......   f<u>ou</u>nd ......ground......

5. Use these words to complete the sentences below.

| loud | mouse | outside | crowd |

The ......crowd...... gave a cheer and waved flags.

The music was very ......loud...... at the concert.

A ......mouse...... is a small animal.

When it started to rain ......outside......, everyone ran inside.

These pages cover two separate sounds: "oy" as in "boy" and "ow" as in "crown." There are two common spelling patterns for each sound: **oy** and

oi for "oy" sound; and **ow** and **ou** for the "ow" sound. Remind children that the letters **ow** can also make the long "o" sound as practiced on page 37.

40

1. Complete these words by adding the letters **wh** or **tw**.

<u>wh</u>eel   <u>tw</u>ig   <u>wh</u>istle

<u>tw</u>ins   <u>tw</u>elve   <u>wh</u>ale

2. Use these words to complete the sentences.

| twenty | wheat | what | twisted |

The strands of hemp were ......twisted...... to make a rope.

......What...... color is the flag?

......Twenty...... is written with the digits 2 and 0.

The ......wheat...... was made into bread.

41

3. The letters **qu** make the "kw" sound. Match each question to its word answer.

What noise does a duck make?   quill
What did ancient writers use to write?   queen
What is a king's wife called?   quiet
What is the opposite of noisy?   quack

4. The letters **ph** make the "f" sound. Circle the letters that make the "f" sound in these words.

ele<u>ph</u>ant   tele<u>ph</u>one   dol<u>ph</u>in

5. Which two letters make the "f" sound?   **ph**
   Which two letters make the "kw" sound?   **qu**

In some consonant blends, such as **wh**, it is very tricky to hear the letters. For others, such as **qu** and **ph**, there are no clues as to the sound they make.

Encourage children to read the words once they have completed the page to further reinforce the spelling–sound connections.

Answers:

42–43 Plurals

46–47 "or" and "au" Sounds

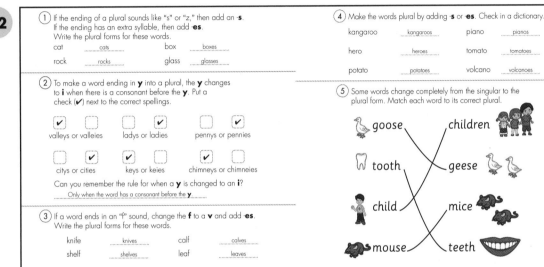

42

① If the ending of a plural sounds like "s" or "z," then add an **-s**.
If the ending has an extra syllable, then add **-es**.
Write the plural forms for these words.

cat — cats   box — boxes

rock — rocks   glass — glasses

② To make a word ending in **y** into a plural, the **y** changes
to **i** when there is a consonant before the **y**. Put a
check (✔) next to the correct spellings.

✔ valleys or valleies   ✔ ladys or ladies   ✔ pennys or pennies

citys or cities ✔   keys or keies ✔   chimneys or chimneies ✔

Can you remember the rule for when a **y** is changed to an **i**?
Only when the word has a consonant before the **y**

③ If a word ends in an "f" sound, change the **f** to a **v** and add **-es**.
Write the plural forms for these words.

knife — knives   calf — calves

shelf — shelves   leaf — leaves

43

④ Make the words plural by adding **-s** or **-es**. Check in a dictionary.

kangaroo — kangaroos   piano — pianos

hero — heroes   tomato — tomatoes

potato — potatoes   volcano — volcanoes

⑤ Some words change completely from the singular to the
plural form. Match each word to its correct plural.

goose — geese
tooth — teeth
child — children
mouse — mice

Check that children know that the term plural refers to
more than one thing. By this stage, they should know
that some plurals can be made by adding the letter **s**
to words. However, depending on the singular word,
an **es** may be added or letters need to be altered
before adding an **s** or **es**. These pages practice these
various rules and also provide some irregular plurals
that don't follow the rules at all.

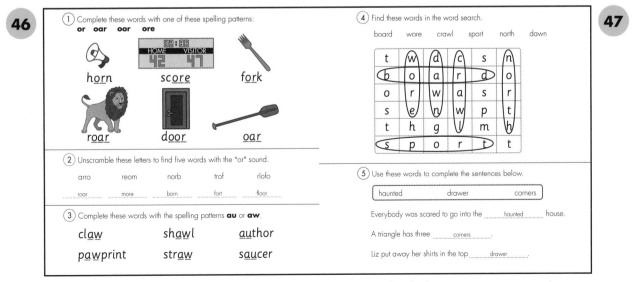

46

① Complete these words with one of these spelling patterns:
or oar oor ore

horn   score   fork

roar   door   oar

② Unscramble these letters to find five words with the "or" sound.

arro — roar   reom — more   norb — born   trof — fort   rlofo — floor

③ Complete these words with the spelling patterns **au** or **aw**.

claw   shawl   author

pawprint   straw   saucer

47

④ Find these words in the word search.

board   wore   crawl   sport   north   dawn

t	w	d	c	s	n
b	o	a	r	d	o
o	r	w	a	s	r
s	e	n	w	p	t
t	h	g	l	m	h
s	p	o	r	t	t

⑤ Use these words to complete the sentences below.

haunted   drawer   corners

Everybody was scared to go into the **haunted** house.

A triangle has three **corners**.

Liz put away her shirts in the top **drawer**.

These pages might be challenging since the
activities require children to practice the many
spelling possibilities for the "or" sound. The "au"
sound is a little easier with the two spelling patterns.

Point out that the letters **au** never come at the
ends of words so for words such as "straw" and
compound words such as "pawprint," the letters
aw will be used.

Answers:

48–49 More Beginning Blends
50–51 Long "oo" Sound

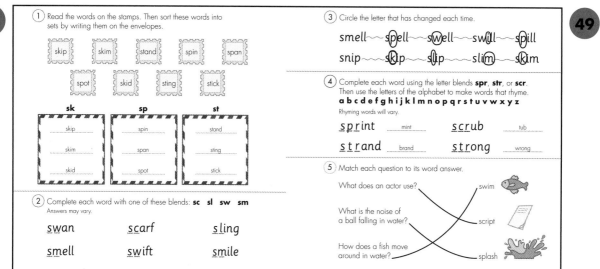

48

① Read the words on the stamps. Then sort these words into sets by writing them on the envelopes.

skip skim stand spin span

spot skid sting stick

sk
skip
skim
skid

sp
spin
span
spot

st
stand
sting
stick

② Complete each word with one of these blends: **sc sl sw sm**
Answers may vary.

swan   scarf   sling

smell   swift   smile

49

③ Circle the letter that has changed each time.

smell — spell — swell — swill — spill

snip — skip — slip — slim — skim

④ Complete each word using the letter blends **spr**, **str**, or **scr**. Then use the letters of the alphabet to make words that rhyme.
abcdefghijklmnopqrstuvwxyz
Rhyming words will vary.

sprint ____ mint   scrub ____ tub

strand ____ brand   strong ____ wrong

⑤ Match each question to its word answer.

What does an actor use? — swim

What is the noise of a ball falling in water? — script

How does a fish move around in water? — splash

Support your child in reading aloud the words on these pages as he/she will then hear how the sound has been made by the blends. For question 2, there are a few options for answers for some of these words e.g. "scan," "swan," "sling," or "swing." Praise your child if he/she notices this and discuss the meanings of the different words.

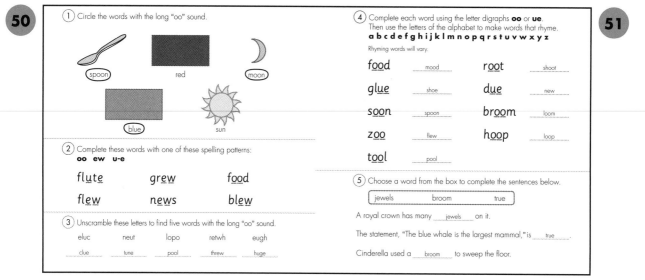

50

① Circle the words with the long "oo" sound.

spoon   red   moon

blue   sun

② Complete these words with one of these spelling patterns:
oo ew u-e

flute   grew   food

flew   news   blew

③ Unscramble these letters to find five words with the long "oo" sound.

eluc   neut   lopo   retwh   eugh

clue   tune   pool   threw   huge

51

④ Complete each word using the letter digraphs **oo** or **ue**. Then use the letters of the alphabet to make words that rhyme.
abcdefghijklmnopqrstuvwxyz
Rhyming words will vary.

food ____ mood   root ____ shoot

glue ____ shoe   due ____ new

soon ____ spoon   broom ____ loom

zoo ____ flew   hoop ____ loop

tool ____ pool

⑤ Choose a word from the box to complete the sentences below.

| jewels | broom | true |

A royal crown has many ____ jewels ____ on it.

The statement, "The blue whale is the largest mammal," is ____ true ____

Cinderella used a ____ broom ____ to sweep the floor.

The long "oo" sound can also be known as the long "u" sound. The sound is represented by a number of spelling patterns that are useful for children to know. Point out that the letters **oo** rarely are used at the ends of words but **ew** often does. For question 3, first find the letters for the spelling pattern and then fit the other letters around it.

Answers:

52–53 Short "oo" Sound

54–55 Silent Letters

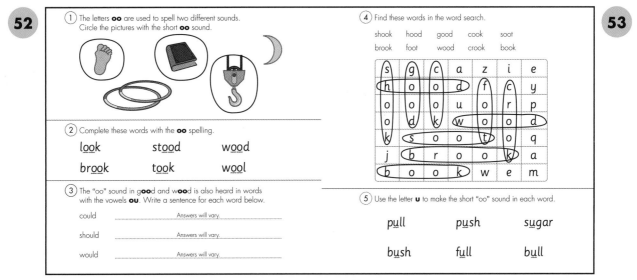

52

① The letters **oo** are used to spell two different sounds. Circle the pictures with the short **oo** sound.

② Complete these words with the **oo** spelling.

look   stood   wood

brook   took   wool

③ The "oo" sound in g**oo**d and w**oo**d is also heard in words with the vowels **ou**. Write a sentence for each word below.

could   Answers will vary.

should   Answers will vary.

would   Answers will vary.

53

④ Find these words in the word search.

shook   hood   good   cook   soot
brook   foot   wood   crook   book

⑤ Use the letter **u** to make the short "oo" sound in each word.

pull   push   sugar

bush   full   bull

All the spelling patterns for this short "oo" sound, such as in "push," are used for other sounds too. Check that children are clearly hearing the

difference between the long and short "oo" sounds in the first question. The words in question 3 are very useful and encourage children to learn them.

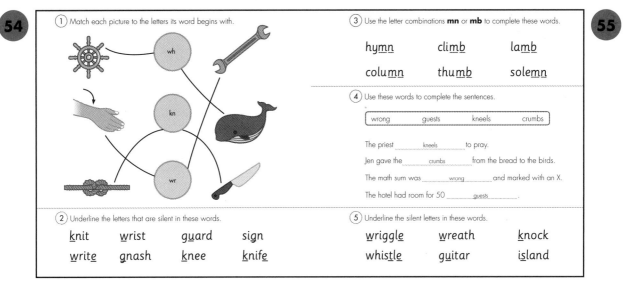

54

① Match each picture to the letters its word begins with.

wh

kn

wr

② Underline the letters that are silent in these words.

knit   wrist   guard   sign

write   gnash   knee   knife

55

③ Use the letter combinations **mn** or **mb** to complete these words.

hymn   climb   lamb

column   thumb   solemn

④ Use these words to complete the sentences.

| wrong | guests | kneels | crumbs |

The priest ___kneels___ to pray.

Jen gave the ___crumbs___ from the bread to the birds.

The math sum was ___wrong___ and marked with an X.

The hotel had room for 50 ___guests___ .

⑤ Underline the silent letters in these words.

wriggle   wreath   knock

whistle   guitar   island

Children need to be aware and watch out for letters that can't be clearly heard in a word. The letters featured on this page are some of the most common ones: **kn**, **gn**, **mn**, **mb**, and **wr**. Point out, when

words with these silent letters appear in the books children are reading. Continue to check that children know how to spell the days of the week as Wednesday is not the only tricky one to spell.

Answers:

56–57 Prefixes and Suffixes
58–59 The Letter **y**

56

1 Add the prefix **un-** to the beginning of each of these words.

un<u>happy</u> un<u>do</u> un<u>load</u>

un<u>fair</u> un<u>lock</u> un<u>wrap</u>

What do you think the prefix **un-** means? not

2 Add the suffix **-less** to the ends of these words.

hope<u>less</u> rest<u>less</u> end<u>less</u>

tire<u>less</u> speech<u>less</u> age<u>less</u>

What do you think the suffix **-less** means? without

3 Complete these words.

enjoy + ment = <u>enjoyment</u> sad + ness = <u>sadness</u>

punish + ment = <u>punishment</u> fit + ness = <u>fitness</u>

agree + ment = <u>agreement</u> dark + ness = <u>darkness</u>

pay + ment = <u>payment</u> ill + ness = <u>illness</u>

57

4 Add the suffix **-ful** to the ends of these words.

use<u>ful</u> cheer<u>ful</u> pain<u>ful</u>

wonder<u>ful</u> care<u>ful</u> mind<u>ful</u>

What do you think the suffix **-ful** means? full of

5 Combine a word from the red box with a word part from the green box to make 10 new words.

| joy | play | glad | open | help | power | cover |

| un- | -less | -ful | -ness |

Count the syllables for each of your new words.

<u>joyful</u> [2] <u>unopen</u> [3]

<u>helpless</u> [2] <u>helpful</u> [2]

<u>gladness</u> [2] <u>powerful</u> [3]

<u>uncover</u> [3] <u>powerless</u> [3]

<u>openness</u> [3] <u>playful</u> [2]

Children are introduced to common prefixes and suffixes in the 2nd Grade. Knowing about these parts added to the beginning and ends of words help children to break down long words into manageable chunks to spell. Also explain to children how prefixes and suffixes can alter the meanings of words, such as "endless," which means to be without an end.

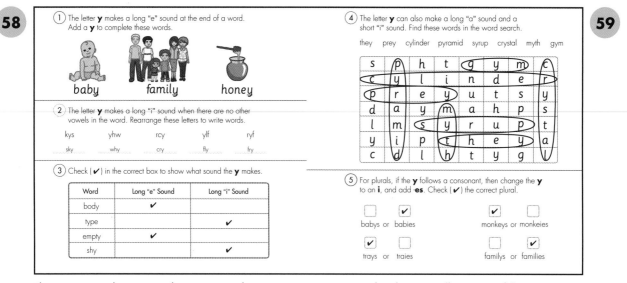

58

1 The letter **y** makes a long "e" sound at the end of a word. Add a **y** to complete these words.

baby family honey

2 The letter **y** makes a long "i" sound when there are no other vowels in the word. Rearrange these letters to write words.

kys yhw rcy ylf ryf

sky why cry fly fry

3 Check (✔) in the correct box to show what sound the **y** makes.

Word	Long "e" Sound	Long "i" Sound
body	✔	
type		✔
empty	✔	
shy		✔

59

4 The letter **y** can also make a long "a" sound and a short "i" sound. Find these words in the word search.

they prey cylinder pyramid syrup crystal myth gym

s	p	h	t	g	y	m	c
c	y	l	i	n	d	e	r
p	r	e	y	u	t	s	y
d	a	y	m	a	h	p	s
l	m	s	y	r	u	p	t
y	i	p	t	h	e	y	a
c	d	l	h	t	y	g	l

5 For plurals, if the **y** follows a consonant, then change the **y** to an **i**, and add **-es**. Check (✔) the correct plural.

□ babys or ✔ babies ✔ monkeys or □ monkeies

✔ trays or □ traies □ familys or ✔ families

These activities demonstrate how even one letter can have two or more different sounds. Question 5 provides further practice about changing the **y** to an **i** before adding many endings. A spelling diary, suggested in the Time Filler, is a useful resource. In it, your child is asked to record the words he/she finds tricky to spell. The pages could follow the content covered in this book.

Answers:

60–61 "j" and "l" Sounds
62–63 Homophones and Homographs

60

1. The letter **j** is never used at the end of a word. Instead, the "j" sound is spelled with **-dge** after the short vowel sounds and **-ge** after all other sounds. Complete these words using the spelling patterns **dge** or **ge**.

cage   bridge   hedge

2. Complete these words with **dge** or **ge**. Then use the words to fill in the sentences.

huge   charge   ledge   fudge   village

The bird sat on the window ledge.

The cell phone was on charge.

The baker made a huge birthday cake flavored with fudge.

Everyone in the village was excited about the mayor's visit.

61

3. Often when the "j" sound comes before **e**, **i**, or **y**, the letter **g** is used. Complete these words using **j** or **g**.

gem   juice   giraffe   jelly

4. The "l" sound at the end of a word has either an **-le** or **-el** spelling. Check (✔) the words that have been spelled correctly.

✔ single   ☐ jungel   ✔ parcel   ☐ simpel
☐ towle   ✔ label   ✔ kennel   ✔ candle

5. Complete these words with **-al** or **-il**.

pencil   sandal   utensil
animal   fossil   petal

These pages show that even some consonant sounds have more than one spelling pattern. The "j" sound made when using the letter **g** can also be known as the soft "g" sound.

This Time Filler is the last of the activities to make other words from the letters of a long word. If your child enjoys this exercise, then do encourage him/her to try it with other words.

62

1. Homophones are words that sound the same but are spelled differently. Link the homophones.

won   see   I   write   real   hear
right   here   sea   one   eye   reel

2. Complete the sentences using these words.

to   too   two   there   their   they're

A letter was sent to the man.

There were two trees in the garden.

The children read their books.

The teacher read her book, too.

They're reading about monkeys.

3. Draw two pictures for each word.

bat   glasses   ring

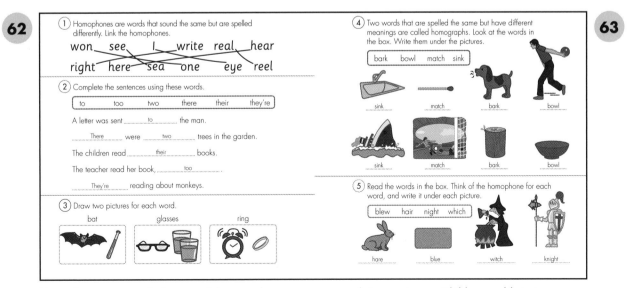

63

4. Two words that are spelled the same but have different meanings are called homographs. Look at the words in the box. Write them under the pictures.

bark   bowl   match   sink

sink   match   bark   bowl
sink   match   bark   bowl

5. Read the words in the box. Think of the homophone for each word, and write it under each picture.

blew   hair   night   which

hare   blue   witch   knight

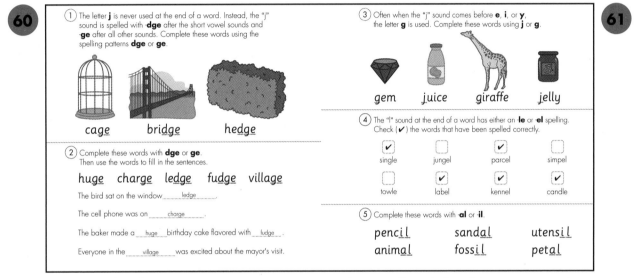

Homophones are words that sound the same but are spelled differently. Homographs are words that are spelled the same but have different meanings. Extend the activity by asking children to put the words into sentences. Children could start a homophone and homograph list and add words as they come across them in their reading and conversation.

Answers:

200 Words Useful
to Learn to Spell

This list of 200 key words for your child to learn to spell includes the words on the Useful Word Lists on pages 20–21, 44–45, and 64–65. Encourage your child to learn these words by looking and saying each word aloud, then covering the word and writing it and then checking. Encourage children to say/write sentences using the words. Once your child is familiar with each group of 10 words then test him/her regularly.

he	can	the	from	left	gave	time	hand	red	January
she	say	that	get	right	give	sing	head	black	February
him	said	they	about	last	live	read	help	blue	March
his	with	their	back	first	long	call	home	white	April
her	want	them	been	second	bring	eat	house	green	May
you	was	then	before	third	best	work	never	brown	June
me	will	this	after	fast	boy	wish	next	yellow	July
my	well	there	again	slow	girl	play	once	gray	August
are	went	these	away	like	round	don't	open	purple	September
for	were	three	always	little	good	can't	close	orange	October
have	one	made	out	soon	any	sit	could	Monday	November
has	two	make	only	stop	many	walk	should	Tuesday	December
had	did	more	often	start	ask	run	would	Wednesday	month
here	do	much	over	take	put	jump	very	Thursday	year
came	down	why	under	tell	pull	skip	every	Friday	school
come	up	where	must	fell	push	climb	other	Saturday	rain
some	so	when	just	find	than	tree	another	Sunday	cloud
see	no	which	your	found	thing	bird	because	today	snow
saw	new	who	old	four	think	animal	yes	tomorrow	wind
how	now	what	own	five	thought	fish	going	yesterday	weather